TOP 10

CORNWALL & DEVON

ROBERT ANDREWS

Top 10 Cornwall and Devon Highlights

The Top 10 of Everything

CONTENTS

Cornwall and Devon Area by Area

Streetsmart

Within each Top 10 list in this book, no hierarchy of quality or popularity is implied. All 10 are, in the editor's opinion, of roughly equal merit.

Front cover and spine *Wheal Coates Tin Mine in St Agnes, Cornwall*
Back cover *The picturesque cove and village of Port Isaac, Cornwall*
Title page *Fishing boats in the harbour at Clovelly, North Devon*

The information in this DK Eyewitness Top 10 Travel Guide is checked regularly. Every effort has been made to ensure that this book is as up-to-date as possible at the time of going to press. Some details, however, such as telephone numbers, opening hours, prices, gallery hanging arrangements and travel information, are liable to change. The publishers cannot accept responsibility for any consequences arising from the use of this book, nor for any material on third party websites, and cannot guarantee that any website address in this book will be a suitable source of travel information. We value the views and suggestions of our readers very highly. Please write to: Publisher, DK Eyewitness Travel Guides, Dorling Kindersley, 80 Strand, London WC2R 0RL, Great Britain, or email travelguides@dk.com

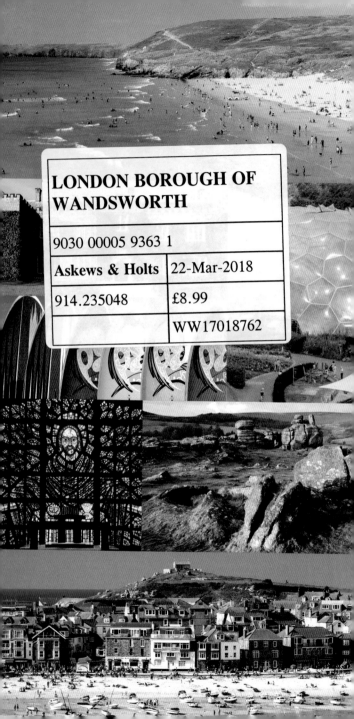

Welcome to
Cornwall and Devon

Rocky coves with white-sand beaches and turquoise waters. Mile-long strands where surfers skim Atlantic breakers. Bleak moorland with standing stones silhouetted against vast skies. Thatched cottages, flower gardens and cream teas. This corner of South West England has all this and more. With Eyewitness Top 10 Cornwall and Devon, it's yours to explore.

The counties of Cornwall and Devon are among the most popular holiday destinations in the UK. Visitors flock here for the spectacular stately homes, whitewashed fishing villages, compelling towns and cities, and traditional seaside resorts like **Torquay** and **Ilfracombe**. Wherever you go, the old-fashioned pleasures of rock-pooling, crabbing and building sandcastles fuse easily with more sophisticated pursuits. Food and drink here is fantastic, with cafés, pubs and restaurants ensuring the region retains its place at the forefront of the movement towards sustainable, local produce. There are vineyards, breweries, ice-cream makers, and even a chilli plantation.

There is something magical about this far-flung peninsula, which has attracted and inspired generations of artists and writers. From Sherlock Holmes seeking diabolical hounds on **Dartmoor** and the riverside tales of *The Wind in the Willows* to Arthurian legend and the works of the **St Ives** and **Newlyn** artists, the landscapes of Cornwall and Devon have been imprinted on the world's imagination.

Whether you're visiting for a weekend or a week, our Top 10 guide brings together the best of Cornwall and Devon, from foodie mecca **Padstow** to the secluded **Isles of Scilly**. The guide gives you tips throughout, such as ideas of what's free and where to go with kids, plus seven easy-to-follow itineraries. Add inspiring photography and detailed maps, and you've got the essential pocket-sized travel companion. **Enjoy the book, and enjoy Cornwall and Devon.**

Clockwise from top: Newquay beach; Eden Project; Dartmoor National Park; St Ives; Buckfast Abbey stained glass; surfboards; Prideaux Place

Exploring Cornwall and Devon

Cornwall and Devon are packed with magnificent beaches, picturesque villages and historic towns, to say nothing of the area's vast moorlands, idyllic countryside and miles of coastal and rural paths. To help you make the most of your visit, here are some ideas for a two-day and seven-day break in the region. To see the Isles of Scilly when time is short, book speedboat transfers in advance.

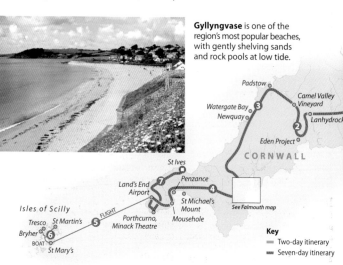

Gyllyngvase is one of the region's most popular beaches, with gently shelving sands and rock pools at low tide.

Key
— Two-day itinerary
— Seven-day itinerary

Two Days in Falmouth

Day ❶
MORNING
Start with the **National Maritime Museum** (see p19), then head up past **Pendennis Castle** (see p19) to sandy **Gyllyngvase Beach** (see p19).

AFTERNOON
Take a pleasure boat trip up the **River Helford**, or make the short drive to **Helford Passage** (see p104) for lunch at the Ferry Boat Inn (see p106). It's then just a five-minute drive to magnificent **Trebah** (see p18).

Day ❷
MORNING
Visit **Falmouth Art Gallery** (see p19), then browse the antique shops before catching a ferry to **St Mawes** (see p19) for a fish and chip lunch.

AFTERNOON
From St Mawes, follow the path along the banks of the River Fal to the subtropical gardens of the church of **St-Just-in-Roseland** (see p43).

Seven Days in Devon and Cornwall

Day ❶
Explore magnificent **Exeter Cathedral** (see pp24–5), with its gloriously intricate Gothic façade and breathtaking fan-vaulting, then drive to the idyllic Dartmoor village of **Widecombe-in-the-Moor** (see p16) for lunch. For some more atmospheric moorland scenery, visit the evocative Bronze Age village of **Grimspound** (see p17), then head to pretty **Dartmeet** (see p17) at the meeting point of the East and West Dart rivers.

beaches of Gyllyngvase, Swanpool and Maenporth, stopping for lunch at a café and a swim if the weather is good. Continue inland to spend a couple of hours at lush **Trebah** (see p18). Drive to Penzance to see **St Michael's Mount** (see pp32–3) at sunset, then head to the idyllic fishing village of **Mousehole** (see p33) for dinner.

Day ❺
Take a 15-minute flight from Land's End airport to the **Isles of Scilly** (see pp26–7). Transfer by speedboat to Tresco, explore the **Tresco Abbey Garden** (see p27), then stop for lunch at the **New Inn** (see p106). Catch a ferry to sparsely inhabited **Bryher** (see p26), and follow the coast path to Hell Bay with its Atlantic breakers. Stay overnight here or return to Tresco.

Day ❻
Take a boat to **St Martin's** (see pp26–7) and snorkel with seals or walk the sandy beaches, then catch a boat to St Mary's for lunch with a view at **Juliet's Garden** (see p107). See shipwreck finds at the **Isles of Scilly Museum** (see p26) before returning to Land's End.

Day ❼
Drive to the white sands of **Porthcurno** and see the **Minack Theatre** (see pp28–9), an open-air amphitheatre carved into the granite cliffs. Head to **St Ives** (see pp30–31) to see the paintings and sculptures held at the Tate and other galleries. Dine at the **Pedn Olva** (see p106), a hotel restaurant perched between the two beaches.

Day ❷
Drive to Victorian **Lanhydrock** (see pp12–13), for a fascinating insight into life in a country house, then move on to the **Eden Project** (see pp14–15). After lunch in one of its cafés, devote the afternoon to the vast Rainforest and Mediterranean biomes.

Day ❸
Drive to the **Camel Valley Vineyard** (see p89), where you can taste and buy fantastic wines. Head on to the fishing village of **Padstow** (see pp34–35), Cornwall's most famous foodie destination, and perhaps treat yourself to a seafood banquet at Rick Stein's flagship Seafood Restaurant. After lunch, follow the coast road to **Newquay** (see p90), with its dramatic cliffs and sweeping sands, making a stop at the surfer's haven, **Watergate Bay** (see p52). Drive on to Falmouth.

Day ❹
Get a taste of **Falmouth** (see pp18–19) and Cornwall's seafaring past at the **National Maritime Museum** (see p19), then follow the coastal route past the

Hewn into the cliffs, Minack Theatre provides a stunning natural backdrop.

Top 10 Cornwall and Devon Highlights

Exeter Cathedral's magnificent rib-vaulted nave

Cornwall and Devon Highlights

The Southwest peninsula holds some of Britain's most forbidding moorland, dramatic coastline and enticing beaches. Its history, from Celtic to Victorian times, is evident in its castles and stately homes, while a range of outdoor activities provide year-round entertainment for the whole family. Equally famed for their tranquillity and soul-stirring views, Cornwall and Devon make ideal holiday destinations.

1 Lanhydrock
This impressive 17th-century mansion, set amid gardens and parkland, is filled with Jacobean art and Victorian furnishings *(see pp12–13)*.

2 Eden Project
Conservation is made fun at this wide-ranging exploration of the plant world, dominated by two giant greenhouses. Summer concerts, winter ice-skating and several cafés and restaurants serving great food enhance its appeal *(see pp14–16)*.

3 Dartmoor
A range of activities is possible on this bleak expanse of moorland, which is complemented by grand houses and cosy villages sheltering thatched pubs *(see pp16–17)*.

4 Falmouth
Falmouth is a historic port and vibrant university town magnificently located on the Fal Estuary. It is home to sandy beaches, bustling art galleries and the fascinating National Maritime Museum *(see pp18–19)*.

Boscastle
Camelford
Padstow
10
Bodmin Moor
Wadebridge
Bodmin
A38
CORNWALL
Newquay
Lanhydrock 1
Eden Project 2 St Blazey
St Agnes
A30
A39
St Austell
Fowey
Redruth
Truro
A390
Mevagissey
8
St Ives • Hayle
Camborne
Penzance
9 9
A394
A394
4 St Mawes
St Michael's Mount
Helston
Falmouth
7
St Keverne
Porthcurno and the Minack Theatre
A3083
6 Isles of Scilly
32 km (20 miles)
Lizard

5 Exeter
Rising from the River Exe, the capital of Devon has a strong historical flavour, not least in its cathedral. It also has a buzzing and vibrant contemporary cultural life (see pp22–5).

6 Isles of Scilly
The islands of this windswept Atlantic archipelago are beautiful, unspoiled, and among the most remote places in Britain (see pp26–7).

7 Porthcurno and the Minack Theatre
Porthcurno's outdoor attractions include a sandy beach between high cliffs and the open-air Minack Theatre, cut out of the rock (see pp28–9).

8 St Ives
Home to the Tate St Ives gallery, this seaside town has a thriving arts scene, sandy beaches and excellent restaurants (see pp30–31).

9 Penzance and St Michael's Mount
The region's most westerly town is home to two superb galleries and is close to St Michael's Mount, a spectacular fortified house crowning an island (see pp32–3).

10 Padstow
As well as its famous restaurants, this fishing port boasts beaches, historic houses and a popular cycle trail (see pp34–5).

🔟 ⭐ Lanhydrock

This magnificent 17th-century mansion in the Fowey Valley is one of England's grandest country houses. Built by a rich merchant, Sir Richard Robartes, and reconstructed in 1881 following a disastrous fire, it remained in the same family until the National Trust took it over in 1953. Though parts of the Jacobean building survived, notably its famous Long Gallery, the dominant style is that of the High Victorian era. Some 50 visitable rooms offer a glimpse into life inside a stately home, from the huge kitchens to Lady Robartes' boudoir.

1 The Gatehouse
This impressive pinnacled structure was built around 1650 **(below)**. The main room on the upper storey was used to entertain ladies while the men hunted. It leads into the Topiary Courtyard.

Lanhydrock

❽ ❹ ❻ ❸ ❾
❺
❼
❿
❶ ❷

2 The Gardens
The clipped yew trees and geometric flowerbeds are striking **(above)**, but it is the magnolias in the shrub garden for which the estate's gardens are most renowned.

3 St Hydroc Church
Dedicated to an Irish missionary, the church adjoining the house dates from the 15th century. A plaster panel in the north aisle displays the arms of King James I and is dated 1621.

4 Captain Tommy's Bedroom
A suitcase **(below)** kept on the cast-iron bed contains the personal items of Thomas Agar-Robartes, who died at the Battle of Loos in 1915.

6 The Dining Room

Decorated with stunning blue-and-gilt wallpaper designed by William Morris, the dining room is dominated by a table set for a formal meal as it would have been in Victorian times **(left)**.

7 The Billiard Room

This spacious room exudes the spirit of the leisured life of the gentry with its billiard table and tiger skin set against oak panelling. Old school photos and other such mementos line the walls.

8 The Kitchen

At the heart of the building is the main kitchen where the cook and servants worked. Its vast interior resembles a church, with soaring rafters and a gabled roof.

BELOW STAIRS

More than any other house of its period, Lanhydrock provides an intriguing insight into how a grand mansion operated. Passages lead from the main kitchen, with its elaborate ranges and gleaming copper, to sculleries, larders, a bakehouse and a dairy. At the top of the house are the nurseries and the servants' modest quarters, a stark contrast to the lavish bedrooms of the owners of the house.

9 The Long Gallery

Lanhydrock's pièce de résistance, occupying the entire first floor of the north wing, is its remarkable plaster ceiling which illustrates stories from the Old Testament.

5 The Nursery Wing

A whole suite of rooms was set aside for bringing up the younger family members. The nursery itself is crowded with a large doll's house and a rocking horse, among many other toys.

10 Woodland Walks

The woods and parkland of the estate are lovely to explore. You can enjoy the exuberant birdlife and, in spring, expanses of bluebells **(above)** and daffodils.

NEED TO KNOW

MAP D4 ■ Near Bodmin, Cornwall ■ 01208 265950 ■ www.nationaltrust.org.uk

Open house: Apr–Sep: 11am–5:30pm daily; Mar & Oct: 11am–5pm daily;

Dec: 11am–4pm daily; garden Apr–Oct 10am–5:30pm daily; Nov–Mar: 10am–4pm daily

Adm £13.55, child £6.75, family £33.85; grounds £8.25, child £4.10

■ Enjoy a great view from the gatehouse stairs. Free garden tours run from here daily.

■ There is the Servants' Hall restaurant in the house and a snack bar in the stables.

TOP 10 ★ Eden Project

A china clay pit transformed to house two giant conservatories and extensive outdoor planting, the Eden Project is an innovative exploration of the plant world and human interaction with it. The grand spectacle of the place grabs the attention, but the Eden Project has a serious agenda, warning of the fragility of Earth's ecosystem through talks and workshops. The educational element never stifles the sense of fun. In summer, this is one of the region's best open-air concert venues, while in winter the arena becomes an ice rink.

3 Mediterranean Biome

The smaller of the two indoor biomes **(left)** houses plants from the Mediterranean, South Africa and southwestern America. Exhibits include orange trees, olives and vividly coloured flowers.

5 The Spiral Garden

This innovative garden, designed with children in mind, explores patterns in nature. Visitors are encouraged to touch the plants, roll on the grass and clamber through tunnels.

1 Rainforest Biome

Hot and steamy with a waterfall coursing through it, this luxuriant biome re-creates a tropical climate for plants from West Africa, Amazonia and Malaysia.

2 Outside Biome

In this roofless biome, plants are cultivated in Cornwall's temperate climate. Native Cornish flora is found alongside plants from Australasia and Chile.

4 The Core

The message of the Eden Project (mankind's dependence on Earth's resources) is presented with flair at the Core education centre and exhibition venue. The building's design mimics a tree, with Peter Randall-Page's granite sculpture, *Seed* **(right)**, its centrepiece.

6 Eden's Restaurants

The award-winning restaurants here offer globally-inspired cuisine prepared with locally sourced ingredients. There is catering for all diets as well as imaginative children's meals and Cornish cream teas. Eden's restaurants include the Med Terrace, Eden Kitchen and the Pasty Snack Bar.

The vast glass biomes of the Eden Project

7 The Canopy Walkway

Set high above the treetops in the Rainforest Biome, this gives visitors a bird's-eye view, with the stunning biodiversity chandelier overhead **(above)**.

9 Eden's Artworks

The artworks at the Eden Project include specially commissioned temporary exhibits, as well as permanent displays, such as a giant bee **(left)** and the dancing Dionysian figures set within the Mediterranean Biome.

8 Visitor Centre

Adorned with sculptures, including Heather Jansch's *Driftwood Horse* made from driftwood and cork, the Visitor Centre's viewpoint at the top of the pit offers a taste of the marvels to come. From here, the full scale of the place becomes apparent.

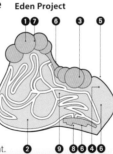

Eden Project

FACTS AND FIGURES

Nearly 60 m (200 ft) deep, the former clay pit required 85,000 tonnes of soil (a mix of china clay and composted waste) to transform it into a horticultural wonderland. The site contains over a million plants of more than 5,000 species. Based on architect R B Fuller's designs, Eden's massive covered biomes are the largest conservatories in the world – the 50-m- (164-ft-) high Rainforest Biome could hold the Tower of London.

10 Eden Sessions

The crowd-pulling "Eden Sessions" held in summer have included memorable gigs by stars such as Lionel Richie, Elton John and Paloma Faith, plus various lesser-known artists.

NEED TO KNOW

MAP D4 ■ Bodelva, Cornwall ■ 01726 811911 ■ www.edenproject.com

Open Apr–Oct: 9:30am–6pm daily; Aug: closes 8pm Mon–Thu; Nov–mid-Mar: 10am–4:30pm Mon–Fri, 9:30am–6pm Sat & Sun; last adm 90 min before closing

Adm £27.50, child £14; lower prices if booked online

■ Eden can be taxing on the feet, but the Land Train provides some relief, especially for the ascent to the exit.

■ There is no need to bring food here – Eden has many good-quality restaurants and cafés.

🔟 ⭐ **Dartmoor**

Southern England's greatest expanse of wilderness holds a unique fascination – its heather-strewn slopes and rocky tors are haunted by legends and scattered with 3,000-year-old relics. Hemmed in by the moorland are some of Devon's grandest mansions and prettiest villages. The towns of Okehampton and Tavistock hold markets and museums, while Princetown has information on organized walks on a network of paths accessing the remotest areas. There is plenty of scope for cycling and horse riding, or caving, canoeing and climbing.

① Fingle Bridge
Crowds home in on this bridge over the River Teign, but you can find peace on the paths that weave along the shaded banks. The Fingle Bridge Inn provides welcome drinks and snacks **(below)**.

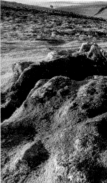

② Okehampton Castle
A tall, seemingly tottering tower greets visitors as they approach this ancient Norman construction, surrounded by woodland. Inside the castle, you can view the remains of the gatehouse, the keep and the Great Hall.

④ Museum of Dartmoor Life
This museum provides a fascinating insight into the lives of the moor's inhabitants, past and present. Displays include everything from antique agricultural tools and farm pick-ups to a Bronze Age hut and domestic bric-a-brac.

⑤ Merrivale Rows
Trailing across moorland west of Princetown, these stones give an idea of the kind of prehistoric society that lived here. The complex includes huts and granite tombs.

③ Widecombe-in-the-Moor
This idyllic village is known for its pinnacled church tower **(below)**, a prominent local landmark, and for the famous folk ditty, *Widecombe Fair*.

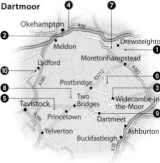

Dartmoor

Okehampton
Meldon
Lydford
Postbridge
Two Bridges
Tavistock
Princetown
Yelverton
Drewsteighto
Moretonhampstead
Widecombe-in-the-Moor
Dartmeet
Ashburton
Buckfastleigh

8 Wistman's Wood

A couple of miles from the road, close to Two Bridges, this tangled wood is a remnant from the time when the moor was completely forested. The ancient, moss-covered trunks make a fantastically atmospheric spot for a picnic **(left)**.

THE HOUND OF THE BASKERVILLES

This Conan Doyle tale has various possible sources. Local legends tell of a huntsman who terrorized the Devon countryside while accompanied by a pack of red-eyed hounds. Another inspiration may be the legend of the Black Dog of Dartmoor, said to chase late-night travellers all the way to their destination.

10 Lydford Gorge

In this remote ravine, the River Lyd tumbles over the 30-m (100-ft) White Lady Waterfall and through dense vegetation that shelters wildlife.

6 Grimspound

To the north of Widecombe, these circular prehistoric huts surrounded by a thick wall **(above)** are thought to have been the inspiration for the Bronze Age village where Sherlock Holmes camped in the novel *The Hound of the Baskervilles*.

7 Castle Drogo

Said to be the last castle built in England, this formidable building was constructed in the early 20th century by architect Edwin Lutyens on the whim of grocery magnate Julius Drewe. The lush grounds lead down to the River Teign.

9 Dartmeet

This is a renowned beauty spot at the junction of the East and West Dart rivers. Nearby is one of Dartmoor's ancient crossing points, the famous clapper bridges **(below)**.

NEED TO KNOW

MAP J4

Okehampton Castle: Glendale Rd, Okehampton; 01837 52844; adm £4.80, child £2.90; www.english-heritage.org.uk

Castle Drogo: Drewsteignton; 01647 433306; open Mar–Oct: 11am–5pm daily; adm £11, child £5.50, family £27.50

Museum of Dartmoor Life: 3 West St, Okehampton; 01837 52295; open Apr–Nov: 10am–4pm Mon–Fri, 10am–1pm Sat; adm £4, child £2, family £10; www.museumof dartmoorlife.org.uk

Lydford Gorge: The Stables, Lydford; 01822 820320; winter access restricted; adm £8.90, child £4.40, family £22.20

Falmouth and the Fal Estuary

A vibrant university town and port, with several sandy beaches, Falmouth owes its existence to having the world's third largest deep harbour. Artists, students, surfers, tourists and refugees from metropolitan life make this the liveliest of Cornwall's towns, with a year-round calendar of festivals. Its multihued Georgian and Victorian homes spill down hillsides, while the main street follows the river, its waters visible through many a café window.

1 Swanpool Beach and Nature Reserve

A sand and shingle beach sheltered by two headlands **(above)**, Swanpool is named after the brackish lagoon behind it, home to a family of swans. There is a small open-air beach café and a pleasant, short walk along the South West Coast Path to the beach of Maenporth.

2 Trebah

Trebah is one of the county's finest gardens **(below)**, set in a lush, subtropical, intriguingly landscaped ravine above the waters of the River Helford. Highlights here include a jungle of gunnera (giant rhubarb).

3 Flushing

This pretty village on the Penryn river, across from Falmouth, was originally settled by Dutch engineers in the 17th century. There are lovely riverside walks, and the crabbing boat arrives with its cargo of fresh crabs most days at around 3pm.

Falmouth and the Fal Estuary

4 Falmouth Docks

For centuries this has been the last port of call for boats crossing the Atlantic, including solo navigators such as Ellen MacArthur. Used by naval ships, cruise liners and commercial vessels, it is best seen from a viewing point below Pendennis Castle.

6 National Maritime Museum

This museum focuses on the maritime history of Cornwall **(left)**, and on the role of small boats in cultures worldwide. Boats range from a fine 19th-century canoe built for the Duke and Duchess of Bedford to international racing yachts.

FAL OYSTERS

The Fal river is the only place in Europe where wild oysters are harvested by a fleet of sailing boats. Harvesting oysters entails dragging a metal dredge along the silty seabed and scraping the oysters into a net. Oyster fishing is strictly regulated and takes place only between 1 October and 31 March.

8 Pendennis Castle

Pendennis, dominated by its four-storey circular keep, was built by Henry VIII in 1540–42 as one of a chain of coastal fortresses **(below)** designed to pro-tect the south coast from European invasion.

5 Trelissick

Set above the River Fal, and accessible by ferry from Falmouth and St Mawes (as well as by road), these colourful gardens also have a gallery showcasing Cornish art.

7 Gyllyngvase Beach

Falmouth's most popular beach is a gently shelving sandy crescent with rock pools at low tide. Gylly Beach Café and water sports add to the appeal.

NEED TO KNOW

MAP C5

National Maritime Museum: Discovery Quay, Falmouth; 01326 313388; open 10am–5pm daily; www.nmmc.co.uk

Falmouth Art Gallery: The Moor; 01326 313863; open 10am–5pm Mon–Sat; www.falmouth artgallery.com

Pendennis Castle: Castle Drive, Falmouth; 01326 316594; open Apr–Oct: 10am–5pm daily; Nov–Mar: times vary; www. english-heritage.org.uk

Trelissick: King Harry, Feock; 01872 862090; open 10:30am–5:30pm daily (mid-Feb–Nov: to 4:30pm); www.nationaltrust.org.uk

Trebah: Mawnan Smith; 01326 252200; open 10am–4pm daily; www. trebahgarden.co.uk

■ The most enjoyable place for seafood and shellfish in Falmouth is The Wheel House *(see p99)*.

■ Much of the Estuary can be explored by boat, with ferries and pleasure boats operating from Falmouth.

9 Falmouth Art Gallery

This small gallery has an outstanding permanent collection ranging from Pre-Raphaelite paintings and engravings of Cornish landscapes by Turner to contemporary prints and children's illustrations.

10 St Mawes

Set in a sheltered corner of the Fal Estuary, and dominated by a castle, this whitewashed village has been an exclusive holiday retreat since Edwardian times.

Following pages St Michael's Mount, Mount's Bay

TOP10 ⭐ Exeter

Rising up from the River Exe and dominated by the twin towers of its cathedral, Exeter holds more historical interest than any other city in the region. The city has a vibrant cultural life, thanks in part to its university students and the Royal Albert Memorial Museum. Its compact centre is walkable, while the Quay is a pleasant spot for a daytime snack. In the evening, pick from one of the city's many restaurants or visit its historic pubs.

1 The Quay
At one time a hardworking harbour, the Quay **(above)** now offers peace and quiet by day, with only a few cafés and crafts and antiques shops. In contrast, the evenings can be lively, with pubs and clubs drawing in the crowds.

2 Along the Exe
Enjoy a tranquil walk or cycle ride along the Exeter Ship Canal and the Exe Estuary, and spot a range of birdlife along the way. Bikes can be hired from the Quay.

3 Quay House
This restored 17th-century building on the quayside now houses a visitor centre with models, paintings and an audiovisual exhibition on the city's history. Regular tours of the city start here.

4 Royal Albert Memorial Museum
As well as its fine art collection, this splendid Victorian Neo-Gothic building contains a number of evocative displays featuring world cultures, local and natural history, costumes and textiles.

5 Stepcote Hill
This steeply sloped medieval lane was once a busy main route. At the bottom, Tudor buildings **(below)** stand alongside one of Exeter's oldest churches, St Mary Steps.

6 Exeter Cathedral

Sheltered within the harmonious Close, the 14th-century Gothic cathedral's most compelling features are its carved, honey-coloured façade (below) and a vaulted nave – the longest in the country.

Exeter

10 St Nicholas Priory

This Benedictine priory survived the Dissolution of the Monasteries and today displays Tudor household items (below). Closed for refurbishment.

7 The Guildhall

Dating from 1330, the Guildhall still serves municipal functions but visitors can pop in to admire the portraits in the grand main chamber.

8 Bill Douglas Cinema Museum

Cinematic memorabilia is displayed in this centre on the university campus. Exhibits range from magic lantern slides to Charlie Chaplin posters and *E.T.* money boxes.

9 Underground Passages

This subterranean network was built in the 14th century to carry water into the city. Guided tours through the tunnels are fascinating.

NEED TO KNOW

Tourist Office:
MAP Q2; Dix's Field, Paris St; 01392 665700; www.visitexeter.com

Exeter Cathedral: **MAP Q2**; Cathedral Close; 01392 285983; open 9am–5pm daily; adm £7.50; www.exeter-cathedral.org.uk

The Guildhall: **MAP P2**; High St; 01392 665500

Bill Douglas Cinema Museum: **MAP N1**; Old Library, Prince of Wales Rd; 01392 724321; www.bdcmuseum.org.uk

Underground Passages: **MAP Q2**; 2 Paris St; 01392 665887; adm £6, child (aged 5–18) £4, family £18

St Nicholas Priory: **MAP P2**; The Mint, off Fore St; 01392 271732; closed for refurbishment

Royal Albert Memorial Museum: **MAP P2**; Queen St; 01392 265858; open 10am–5pm Tue–Sun; www.rammuseum.org.uk

■ Eat at On the Waterfront, set in a 19th-century warehouse at 4–9 The Quay (01392 210590).

Exeter Cathedral

1 Gothic Façade
Apostles, prophets and soldiers jostle for space on the crowded carved West Front of the cathedral. Also look out for depictions of the kings Alfred, Athelstan, Canute, William I and Richard II.

2 Sepulchre of Hugh Courtenay
The cathedral is crammed with tombs, none more eye-catching than the 14th-century sepulchre of Hugh Courtenay, Earl of Devon, and his wife. Their tomb is carved with graceful swans and a lion.

3 Choir
Dominated by a 18-m (60-ft) bishop's throne and a massive organ case, the Choir (or "Quire") holds stalls dating from the 19th century. These feature a series of carvings, such as one that shows an elephant, dating from as far back as the 1250s.

4 Cathedral Close
The lawns surrounding the cathedral are a pleasant place to relax. They are overlooked by an array of historical buildings, including the splendid Elizabethan Mol's Coffee House, which is now a leather goods shop. The remains of a Roman bath house and a Saxon burial site lie beneath the lawns.

Impressive rib-vaulted Gothic ceiling

5 Ceiling
This is the longest unbroken Gothic ceiling in the world. It makes an immediate impression with a dense network of rib-vaulting, shafts and mouldings. One of the ceiling bosses illustrates the murder in 1170 of Thomas à Becket, Archbishop of Canterbury.

Exeter Clock

6 Exeter Clock
The clock in the cathedral's left transept dates from the late 15th century, though the minutes dial was added only in 1759. The sun and moon revolve around the Earth, in the form of a golden ball.

7 Chapter House
From the right transept, a door leads into the Chapter House, originally constructed in the 1220s but mostly rebuilt after a fire in 1413. Beneath the fine timber ceiling stands an array of sculptures from the 20th century. The Chapter House also serves as a popular venue for classical music concerts. You can pick up a leaflet for details.

Lawns at Cathedral Close

8 Plaque to R D Blackmore

Among the tombs and memorials that line the walls of the aisles, one near the door is dedicated to R D Blackmore *(see p48)*, the 19th-century author of the rip-roaring Exmoor romance *Lorna Doone*.

9 The Towers

Dating from the 12th century, the two central towers represent the oldest part of the cathedral. They remain the most conspicuous feature of Exeter's skyline.

Carved angels, Minstrels' Gallery

10 Minstrels' Gallery

High up on the left of the nave a minstrels' gallery from 1350 depicts angels playing musical instruments.

EXETER'S HISTORY

Previously a settlement of the Celtic Dumnonii tribe, Exeter became the most westerly outpost of the Roman Empire in Britain when it was garrisoned in around AD 50–55. Saxon settlement was followed by Danish attacks, but conditions were peaceful under the Norman regime after 1068. The town's position on the River Exe allowed it to become a major outlet for wool shipments. During the Civil War, it became the western headquarters of the Royalists and sheltered Charles I's queen. In the early 20th century, bombing during World War II spared the cathedral, but devastated the historic centre. However, the founding of the University of Exeter in 1955 helped inject new energy into the city, and the Princesshay development has since reversed some of the damage done by shabby postwar reconstruction.

TOP 10 KEY EVENTS IN EXETER'S HISTORY

1 Exeter was fortified by the Romans in AD 50–55.

2 Around 878, the city was re-founded by Alfred the Great, King of Wessex.

3 In 1068, the Normans took control and expanded the wool trade.

4 The countess of Devon diverted the shipping trade to Topsham in the late 13th century.

5 The construction of Exeter Cathedral was completed in 1369.

6 In 1564–66, the Quay and the Ship Canal were constructed.

7 The city sheltered Charles I's queen in 1643, but fell to the Roundheads in 1646.

8 Trade ceased during the Napoleonic wars (1799–15), damaging the local textile industry.

9 World War II bombing flattened the city centre.

10 In 2007, the Princesshay development spearheaded a regeneration project in the historic centre.

Exeter's historic Quay House, located at the water's edge, is home to the city's visitor centre.

TOP 10 ⭐ Isles of Scilly

This archipelago of more than 100 uninhabited and five inhabited islands, scattered in the Atlantic Ocean 45 km (28 miles) off the Cornish coast, boasts some of Europe's most enchanting vistas. Reached by ferry or plane, the Isles of Scilly offer unspoiled white sandy beaches, wild moorland, idyllic harbours and subtropical gardens. Vines, pinks, narcissi and daffodils are cultivated in the mild climate, though an abundance of shipwrecks is testimony to the wild storms that can thrash the islands in the winter months.

New Grimsby, Tresco ①

Overlooking a minuscule port are the ruins of King Charles' castle **(right)**, built by Edward VI, and used as a garrison by Royalist troops during the English Civil War. It was no defence against the Roundheads, who in 1651 simply landed on the other side of the island, and used stone from the castle to build their own fortress, Cromwell's Castle, just below.

② Scilly Flowers, St Martin's

This long-established flower farm specializes in pinks and narcissi grown using traditional methods. Bulb fields and packing sheds are open to visitors.

GIG ROWING

Gig racing with a crew of six rowers and a cox in broad wooden boats is a thriving sport in Cornwall and the Isles of Scilly. Historically, pilot boats would race out to guide ships to the shore through treacherous waters, the first to arrive winning the (lucrative) job. The annual World Pilot Gig championships take place in the Isles of Scilly during the last weekend of April.

③ Isles of Scilly Museum

Finds from shipwrecks form the core of this museum, along with a collection of Bronze and Iron Age artifacts.

④ Sea Kayaking on St Martin's

St Martin's is ideal for sea kayaking, with many islets and islands offshore, as well as plenty of sheltered waters. Kayaks with maps and waterproof pouches are available, along with advice on where to go.

⑤ Holy Vale Vineyard

This vineyard of pinot noir, chardonnay and pinot gris vines had its first vintage in 2014. It offers tours and wine tastings with canapés.

⑥ Bryher and Hell Bay

The most dramatic feature of wild, wind-swept Bryher Island is the Atlantic-thrashed Hell Bay **(below)**, while the usually sheltered Sound between Bryher and Tresco is a pictur-esque place to swim or kayak. Wildlife and bird-watching tours are a great way to explore.

9 Snorkelling with Seals

Carefully guided snorkelling safaris enable you to swim among the colonies of Atlantic grey seals around the uninhabited Eastern Isles. The seals are so accustomed to visitors, they often come up and nibble swimmers' fins.

8 Tresco Abbey Garden

This lush landscaped garden **(above)**, with over 20,000 plants from 80 countries, was created by Augustus Smith, who took on the lease of the islands in the 1830s. Dubbed "Kew with the roof off", it was made possible by the building of huge windbreaks to protect the plants from savage Atlantic winds.

7 St Martin's Vineyard

In the fields of a former flower farm, this intimate vineyard offers tastings of Reichensteiner, Siegerebbe and Gewurztraminer during tours.

The Isles of Scilly

10 Halangy Down Ancient Village

A Bronze Age tomb known as Brant's Carn tops a coastal hill above the Iron Age settlement of Halangy Down **(above)**, which continued to be inhabited until Roman times. Excavations here have revealed 11 interconnected stone houses, each of which would have had a thatched roof.

NEED TO KNOW

New Grimsby, Tresco: **MAP A4**; Tresco; www.english-heritage.co.uk

Scilly Flowers, St Martin's: **MAP B3**; Churchtown Farm, St Martin's; 01720 422169; www.scillyflowers.co.uk

Isles of Scilly Museum: **MAP A4**; Church St, St Mary's; 01720 422337; open Easter– Sep: 10am–4:30pm Mon–Fri, 10am–noon Sat; Oct–Good Friday:

10am–noon Mon–Sat; www.iosmuseum.org

St Martin's Freedom Hire: Higher Town; 07925 762856; www.stmartinsfreedomhire.com

Island Wildlife Tours: 42 Sally Port, St Mary's; 01720 422212; www.islandwildlifetours.co.uk

Holy Vale Vineyard: **MAP B4**; Holy Vale, St Mary's; 01720 420317; open Mar–Oct 12:30pm–4:30pm Mon–Fri; www.holyvalewines.co.uk

St Martin's Vineyard: **MAP B4**; adm £12; www.stmartinsvineyard.co.uk

Tresco Abbey Garden: **MAP A4**; Tresco; 01720 424108; open 10am–4pm daily; www.tresco.co.uk

Halangy Down Ancient Village: **MAP B4**; St Mary's; www.english-heritage.org.uk

Snorkelling with Seals: 01720 422848; www.scillysealssnorkelling.com

TOP10 ⭐ Porthcurno and the Minack Theatre

One of Cornwall's brightest gems is lovely Porthcurno Bay, cupped between cliffs on the southern coast of the Penwith Peninsula. While the village itself is low-key, there are plenty of nearby attractions. The famous open-air Minack Theatre is a unique sight, a magical place to take in some culture and entertainment. Below, the wedge of sandy beach provides amusement by day, while the coast path to either side runs through a landscape managed by the National Trust. Smaller beaches and a scattering of historical relics lie within a short clamber.

⑤ Porthcurno Beach

Porthcurno's beach (left) is among the finest on the Penwith Peninsula. Sheltered by cliffs on either side, the white sand is mixed with tiny shell fragments. Coastal paths lead to Porth Chapel and Pedn Vounder beaches.

① Minack Theatre

On the steep cliffs above Porthcurno stands the region's famous amphitheatre, set into the rock. In summer, you can attend a variety of theatrical performances.

② Minack Theatre Exhibition Centre

This exhibition centre tells the remarkable story of the creation of the Minack, which was the brainchild of Rowena Cade in the 1930s.

⑥ Treryn Dinas Iron Age Fort

Logan Rock forms part of an Iron Age promontory fort. The few traces that can still be seen include four ramparts and the remains of stone houses within a ditch across the promontory.

The Minack's Rockeries and Garden ③

The rockeries and gardens surrounding the theatre have become an attraction in their own right. The selection of plants – colourful succulents and hardy shrubs (right) – is based on plans by Rowena Cade, the Minack's founder.

THE BUILDING OF THE MINACK

Rowena Cade bought the Minack headland for £100. She built a house here and began organizing amateur theatre productions for friends in the 1920s. From this she developed the more ambitious idea of an open-air theatre, and in 1932 the first production – *The Tempest* – was staged. Rowena Cade continued to improve the site until her death in 1983.

④ Pedn Vounder's White Pyramid

Halfway along the path to Logan Rock, visitors will come across this peculiar structure (left), placed here in the 1950s to mark the termination of a telegraph cable that once reached across the Channel to France.

⑨ The View from the Minack

In sunny weather, you could imagine yourself on Italy's Amalfi coast as you take in the inspiring view from this cliffside theatre. The jagged headland forms a truly magnificent backdrop to performances, which run for 17 weeks of the year.

⑩ Porthcurno Telegraph Museum

In 1870, an undersea cable was laid between North America and Porthcurno. A museum exploring the history of the telegraph system now occupies the former terminus, set within a network of underground tunnels.

⑦ Minack Café

No spot is more panoramic for a snack than this lovely coffee shop, perched on a cliff edge within the complex. It is open only to visitors and playgoers.

⑧ Logan Rock

The 70-tonne rock stands on an outcrop on the eastern edge of Porthcurno Bay **(right)**. It was once said to rock from side to side, but has not moved since 1824.

NEED TO KNOW

MAP A6

Minack Theatre: Porthcurno; 01736 810694; opening hours vary, check online; adm £5, under-16s £2.50, under-11s 50p; www.minack.com

Minack Box Office: 01736 810181; tickets £10–£14, under-16s £5–£7

Porthcurno Telegraph Museum: Porthcurno; 01736 810966; open Apr–Sep: 10am–5pm daily; adm adult £8.95, child £5, concession £7.50, family £24.95; www.telegraphmuseum.org

■ Visitors with mobility problems can book the viewing platform above the auditorium.

■ Snacks are available at the Minack Coffee Shop. Alternatively, head to the Porthcurno Beach Café for baguettes and flapjacks (01736 810834).

■ The theatre is a real suntrap so if you are visiting in hot weather be sure to wear sun cream and take plenty of water.

⭐ St Ives

St Ives is like nowhere else in Britain. Its intricate mesh of lanes backs onto a bustling quayside and a quartet of sandy beaches, with lovely views at every turn. As well as the region's premier art gallery, the Tate St Ives, the town has smaller galleries displaying local scenes and landscapes that attest to its role as an artists' hub. There is a dense concentration of bars and restaurants, hotels and B&Bs, many squeezed into tiny cottages.

1 St Ives Museum

Finding this museum in the maze of back streets is like discovering a treasure chest. The quirky collection covers every aspect of local history, from geology and archaeology to mining, farming and shipwrecks.

3 Tate St Ives

Very few British galleries have such a striking setting as this, overlooking Porthmeor Beach. The design of its circular entrance recalls the gasworks that once stood here **(right)**. Inside, displays focus on the work of local artists.

2 St Ia

This 15th-century parish church **(below)** is dedicated to St Ia, the missionary after whom the town is probably named. Its features include a wagon roof and a granite font.

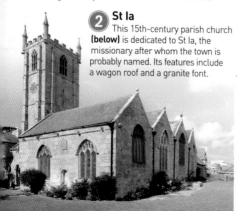

4 Barbara Hepworth Museum and Sculpture Garden

Sculptor Barbara Hepworth was central to the mid-20th-century arts scene in St Ives. Her studio is one of the most compelling galleries in Cornwall, showing her mainly abstract works. Larger pieces are found in the garden *(see p102)*.

⑤ Porthminster Beach

The largest of St Ives' beaches **(below)** always has space for swimming or lounging, and is very popular with sand sculptors. Also here is the famous Porthminster Beach Café (see p107).

⑦ St Ives Society of Artists Gallery

Housed in the former Mariners Church, this gallery is a good place in which to take in contemporary work by the Society's members. The Mariners Gallery in the former crypt also holds private exhibitions.

St Ives

⑥ St Ives September Festival

This boisterous, 15-day festival features comedy, tribute bands, local folk music and African dance. Many pubs also host music, which you can often hear for free.

⑧ Porthmeor Beach

Backed by cafés and the façade of the Tate, and with the promontory of the island at its eastern end, Porthmeor is the most accessible St Ives beach. Its firm sand is ideal for castle-building.

ART IN ST IVES

In 1920, potters Bernard Leach and Shoji Hamada set up the Leach Pottery. Several artists followed, including painter Ben Nicholson and sculptor Barbara Hepworth in 1939. Along with later arrivals such as Patrick Heron and Terry Frost, they specialized in abstract work and were strongly influenced by Cornish landscapes.

⑨ Trewyn Subtropical Gardens

In the heart of St Ives, this quiet retreat with banana trees and other subtropical plants is a peaceful spot even in high season, and makes an ideal picnic venue.

⑩ Leach Pottery

Britain's foremost potter, Bernard Leach (1887–1979) established this pottery studio in 1920 to create his Japanese-inspired work **(above)**. Today, you can see exhibitions of his pottery and watch contemporary ceramicists at work.

NEED TO KNOW

MAP B5

Tourist Information: Street-an-Pol; 01736 796297; www.stives-cornwall.co.uk

St Ives Museum: Wheal Dream; 01736 796005

Tate St Ives: Porthmeor Beach; 01736 796226

St Ia: Market Place; www.stiveschurch.org.uk

Barbara Hepworth Museum and Sculpture Garden: Barnoon Hill; 01736

796226; open Mar–Oct: 10am–5:20pm daily; Nov–Feb: 10am–4:20pm Tue–Sun

St Ives Society of Artists Gallery: Norway Square; 01736 795582

Leach Pottery: Higher Stennack; 01736 799703

■ St Ives is a driver's nightmare. Central car parks are Barnoon, above the Tate, or at the station.

■ The Tate's rooftop café has fantastic panoramas.

TOP 10 ⭐ Penzance and St Michael's Mount

The port of Penzance sits at the northern end of Mount's Bay. Georgian buildings characterize much of the town, though the Jubilee seawater lido is pure Art Deco. The town has two excellent galleries that continue the tradition of the colony of artists who settled in neighbouring Newlyn. Across Mount's Bay, the tiny castle-crowned island of St Michael's Mount is linked to the mainland by a causeway at low tide. It was granted to Benedictine monks from Mont-St-Michel, Normandy, by Edward the Confessor in the 11th century.

3 Market Jew Street

Penzance's main street derives its name from the Cornish "Marghas Yow", meaning Thursday Market. At its top is the domed Market House.

4 Chapel Street

Chapel Street has some of Penzance's comeliest buildings, including the Egyptian House (left) dating from 1830. Across the road is the Union Hotel, featuring a minstrels' gallery.

5 The Exchange

Behind its glass façade, the town's old telephone exchange boasts the largest single exhibition space within 300 km (180 miles).

Penzance and St Michael's Mount

1 Newlyn

Within walking distance of Penzance, Newlyn is a busy fishing port with a thriving early-morning fish market. Attractions include the Newlyn Art Gallery, which displays contemporary art (see p104).

2 The Castle

Originally a Benedictine priory, the castle (below) was sold, along with the island, to John St Aubyn after the Civil War, and remains a stately family home. The Great Hall is known as the Chevy Chase Room after the frieze depicting hunting scenes described in the eponymous Scottish Ballad.

6 Mousehole

Mousehole (pronounced "mowzel") is a pretty village south of Newlyn, with tiers of whitewashed and granite cottages above a sheltered harbour **(above)**.

7 The Causeway, St Michael's Mount

Set off the Marazion coast, the promontory on which St Michael's Mount stands can be reached by boat, but at low tide you can walk across a causeway.

8 Jubilee Pool

Located off Penzance's harbour, this sleek and triangular lido dates back to 1935. It offers open-air, sea-water swimming for all ages during the summer.

9 Penlee House

The Newlyn school of artists, who settled in the area in the late 19th century *(see p41)*, are well represented in this Victorian gallery and museum set within a park. The exhibits reflect the town's fishing and mining heritage.

10 The Chapel, St Michael's Mount

From the Blue Drawing Room, a door leads into the Priory Church **(left)** at the island's summit. Still regularly used for services, it has memorials to the St Aubyn family, who have lived in the castle since 1659.

ST MICHAEL'S WAY

St Michael's Way, which runs for 20 km (12 miles) from Lelant, near St Ives, to the island, is part of a vast European network of pilgrim routes to Santiago de Compostela in Spain. It is thought to have been used by pilgrims from Ireland and Wales who felt it safer to abandon their ships and walk across the peninsula, rather than to navigate the treacherous waters around Land's End.

NEED TO KNOW
MAP B5

Tourist Information: Station Approach, Penzance; 01736 335530; www.love penzance.co.uk

Newlyn Art Gallery: **MAP A5**; New Rd, Newlyn; 01736 363715; www.newlynartgallery. co.uk

St Michael's Mount: Marazion; 01736 710265; adm castle: £9.50, family £23.50; adm garden: £7; child £3.50; ferry £2 each way, child £1; www. stmichaelsmount.co.uk

The Exchange: Princes St, Penzance; 01736 363715

Jubilee Pool: Promenade, Penzance; 01736 369224; adm; www.jubileepool. co.uk

Penlee House: Morrab Rd, Penzance; 01736 363625; adm £4.50, free Sat; www.penlee house.org.uk

■ The terrace and gardens of the castle are worth a wander and offer excellent views.

TOP 10 ⭐ Padstow

Tucked into the Camel Estuary, Padstow is one of Cornwall's most attractive ports. Lively and smart, it is well-placed for beaches, with Daymer, Polzeath, Trevone and Constantine all within easy reach. This is mainly a fishing port whose catch is taken daily to auctions at Brixham and Newlyn, though plenty also ends up in local eateries. Foodies know the town as the domain of celebrity seafood chef Rick Stein, who has raised Padstow's profile with his luxury hotels and seafood restaurants, which are among the best in the country.

1 Prideaux Place

On a hill overlooking the town, this Elizabethan manor house **(above)** has richly furnished rooms and superlative plasterwork. Outside are formal gardens and a deer park.

2 Rick Stein's Restaurants

As well as the delightful Seafood Restaurant, Stein runs five boutique hotels, a bar, a café, a bistro, a patisserie, a fish and chip shop, a seafood bar and a cooking school in Padstow.

3 Padstow Harbour

The town's inner harbour **(above)** is where crowds gather to see the catch being brought in. On the quayside is Abbey House, Padstow's oldest building. Boat trips explore the estuary.

Padstow

4 Obby Oss

One of Cornwall's most flamboyant festivals **(left)** takes place annually on 1 or 2 May. Processions around the town are led by the costumed figure of the Obby Oss (see p68).

5 National Lobster Hatchery

Get close to various crustaceans at this exhibit, where tanks hold spider crabs, crayfish and sponges, and range from tiny baby lobsters to the resident giants **(right)**.

7 Saints Way

Crossing the peninsula to Fowey, this 45-km (28-mile) trail traces the route taken by pilgrims. It follows both ancient footpaths and country lanes from its starting point at St Petroc's Church.

8 St Petroc's Church

Padstow was once known as Petrocstowe, after the missionary St Petroc, who is said to have crossed the Irish Sea on a cabbage leaf. The church is famous for the Prideaux-Brune memorial and for its magnificent 15th- or 16th-century font carved from Catacleuse stone.

THE OBBY OSS TALE

The festival's origins are now lost but it includes elements of many other May Day festivities. Controlled by club-wielding "Teazers", the Obby Oss figures, in twirling hooped gowns, are probably intended to drive winter away, while the white-clothed escorts represent spring. The festivities begin the night before, when Blue Ribbon Oss leaves the Golden Lion pub.

10 Padstow Museum

This museum in the old station building is packed with archaeological items, nautical models, old photos and an Obby Oss costume.

6 Camel Trail

This is Cornwall's finest walking and cycling route, which follows a disused railway line alongside the River Camel for more than 34 km (21 miles). You can rent bikes in Padstow.

9 Camel Estuary

The main river on Cornwall's north coast, the Camel is a haven for migrant wading birds that feed on the fertile mudflats **(above)**. Passenger ferries cross the estuary from Padstow to Rock.

NEED TO KNOW

MAP D3

Tourist Information: North Quay; 01841 533449

Prideaux Place: 01841 532411; open Apr–Sep: 1:30–5pm Sun–Thu, last tour 4pm; adm house: £9; adm grounds: £4; www. prideauxplace.co.uk

National Lobster Hatchery: South Quay; 01841 533877; open 10am daily; adm £3.95

St Petroc's Church: Church St; 01841 533776

Padstow Museum: Market Place; open Apr–Oct: 10:30am–4:30pm Mon–Fri, 10:30am–1pm

Sat; www.padstow museum.co.uk

■ Enquire at the tourist information centre about open-air brass band concerts, which are performed in Padstow most Sundays and during some weekdays throughout the summer.

The Top 10 of Everything

**Sheltered golden sands at
Porthcurno Bay, Cornwall**

TOP10 Moments in History

Hingston Hill stone circle and row (Down Tor), Dartmoor

1 2200–1700 BC: Gold Rush
It is thought that up to 200 kg (450 lb) of gold was extracted from Cornwall and West Devon's rivers, and exported, along with tin, to Europe and Ireland. Settlements, such as Grimspound on Dartmoor, and numerous stone circles and standing stones can still be seen.

2 AD 50–55: Roman Invasion
The Romans established a strong garrison in Exeter and it was assumed they did not reach further west into the Celtic tribes' territory. However, the 2016 discovery of a stretch of Roman road near Newton Abbot suggests that Roman influence may have reached as far as Totnes.

3 6th and 7th Centuries: Anglo-Saxon Villages
During Roman withdrawal, Saxon tribes began to settle in the region, but made little headway against the Celtic tribes, whose strongholds were concentrated in Cornwall. Arthurian legends probably derive from the exploits of one of the Celtic chieftains, who resisted the Anglo-Saxons.

4 11th to 16th Centuries: The Wool Industry
Devon's wool industry flourished under the stability of Norman rule. Landowners of fertile inland pastures built mansions and merchants exported produce to Europe from the southern ports, which grew rich.

5 1530s: Dissolution of the Monasteries
The great monastic houses, which wielded huge influence and power, were suppressed by Henry VIII. Some, like the Benedictine abbey of Tavistock, were destroyed; others, such as Buckfast Abbey, became the mansions of wealthy merchants.

6 1558–1603: The Elizabethan Era
Devon became a strategic region during the contest against Spain. Exeter and Plymouth, in particular, were key military and naval bases. The western seaports benefited from the expansion of transatlantic trade, and the first English colonists of the New World set sail from here.

7 1642–51: The Civil War
Most of the region sided with the Royalists during England's Civil War, though both Exeter and

Battle in the English Civil War

Plymouth originally supported the Roundheads (Parliamentarians). King Charles I defeated the army of the Earl of Essex in 1644, but the Royalists were checked by Thomas Fairfax's army. This eventually led to the fall of Pendennis Castle and Exeter in 1646.

8 18th Century: Tin and Copper Mining

Under the Normans, Cornwall had become Europe's biggest source of tin. A series of scientific advances in the 18th century allowed the tin and copper mining industries to become highly profitable. Copper mining, concentrated around Redruth and Camborne, peaked in the 1840s.

9 1884 Onwards: Artists' Colonies Established

Attracted by the intensity of the light, cheap living costs, the dramatic seascapes and the life of fishing communities, painter Stanhope Forbes settled in Newlyn in 1884 and became the leading figure in an artists' colony known as the Newlyn School. Neighbouring St Ives continues to be an important artistic hub.

Ship at Plymouth, World War II

10 1939–45: World War II

Although most of the West Country was designated safe from German attack and received evacuees from London and the Midlands, Plymouth suffered the worst bombing of any British seaport. Exeter was also targeted in the "Baedeker raids", aimed at cultural centres mentioned in Baedeker guidebooks.

TOP 10 ARTHURIAN SITES

Ruins of Tintagel Castle

1 Tintagel Castle
The most evocative of all Arthurian sights is the castle that is believed to be his birthplace (see p89).

2 Slaughterbridge
MAP E3
This spot on Bodmin Moor is said to be the site of King Arthur's last battle, against his nephew Mordred.

3 Dozmary Pool
MAP E3
It is said that Arthur's famous sword, Excalibur, was thrown here and was received by the Lady of the Lake.

4 The Tristan Stone
MAP E4
This monument marks the grave of Drustanus, identified with Tristan (or Tristram), one of Arthur's knights.

5 Lyonnesse
MAP A6
A fabled land sunk beneath the waves, Lyonnesse is another one of the candidates for Arthur's birthplace.

6 Loe Pool
MAP B6
Like Dozmary Pool, this is a site where Excalibur was believed to have been restored to the Lady of the Lake.

7 Camelford
MAP E3
This town on Bodmin Moor is one of several places identified with Camelot.

8 Castle Dore
An Iron Age hillfort said to have been King Mark of Cornwall's home (see p98).

9 Boscastle
After his last battle, Arthur's body was supposedly transported here (see p90).

10 Castle an Dinas
MAP D4
This hillfort outside St Columb Major is believed to be Arthur's hunting lodge.

TOP 10 Museums

1 National Maritime Museum, Cornwall

This museum displays boats from around the world, nautical equipment, interactive displays and marine art. The centrepiece is the grand Flotilla Gallery, where small craft hang from the roof *(see p19)*.

2 Overbeck's Museum

Scientist Otto Overbeck lived in this house until 1937. Many of his more eccentric inventions, such as a "rejuvenating machine", share space with exhibits on local history. The garden offers superb views *(see p82)*.

Exhibit at Overbeck's Museum

3 National Marine Aquarium

MAP Q6 ■ Coxside, Plymouth ■ 08448 937938 ■ Open 10am–5pm daily ■ Adm ■ www.national-aquarium.co.uk

Part traditional aquarium and part 21st-century museum, this complex presents an awe-inspiring survey of ocean life. There are more than 50 live exhibits, which together contain some 4,000 examples of marine life.

4 Royal Albert Memorial Museum

Among the displays at Exeter's largest museum are the clocks and silverware for which the city was well-known. Sladen's study, named after the echinoderm expert, holds one of the largest collections of starfish and sea urchins in the world *(see p22)*.

5 The Museum of Witchcraft and Magic

MAP E2 ■ The Harbour, Boscastle ■ 01840 250111 ■ Open Apr–Oct: 10:30am–6pm Mon–Sat (from 11:30am Sun) ■ Adm ■ www.museumof witchcraftandmagic.co.uk

This small museum houses everything there is to know about witchcraft and Europe's relationship with magic, including the history of local folk magic.

6 Royal Cornwall Museum

Cornwall's county museum covers local geology and culture with collections of insects alongside Roman coins. Buddhist figures from Burma and an unwrapped Egyptian mummy are also on show *(see p95)*.

Underwater display at the National Marine Aquarium

7 Museum of Barnstaple and North Devon

This museum is the perfect place to learn about North Devon's history. Exhibits include locally minted Saxon coins, a 17th-century kiln and local pottery. Natural history is also well represented and part of the museum is devoted to local militaria *(see p73)*.

8 Museum of Dartmoor Life

Housed in a former granary, this museum illustrates aspects of the moor and its inhabitants, from prehistoric hut-dwellers to the tin-mining communities *(see p16)*.

Museum of Dartmoor Life

9 Fairlynch Museum

Fossils, prehistoric flints, 18th-century costumes, and a range of lace and toys help to create a picture of life in South Devon through the ages. The museum building is fascinating in itself – a *cottage orné* – built by a local shipowner *(see p82)*.

10 Helston Folk Museum

MAP B5 ■ Market Place, Helston ■ 01326 564027
■ Open 10am–4pm Mon–Sat
■ www.helstonmuseum.co.uk

This museum focuses on the social history of Helston and the Lizard Peninsula, with sections dedicated to costume, telegraphy pioneer Marconi and the locally born boxing champion Bob Fitzsimmons (1863–1917).

TOP 10 ART GALLERIES

Visitors at the Penlee House Gallery

1 Tate St Ives
This is a superb collection of works by well-known 20th-century and contemporary artists, all with a strong connection to Cornwall *(see p30)*.

2 The Exchange
Penzance's former telephone exchange now puts on a range of inspiring contemporary art shows *(see p32)*.

3 Newlyn Art Gallery
Exhibitions by national and international artists, with a focus on painting and drawing *(see pp32–3)*.

4 Burton Art Gallery and Museum
Paintings and prized local slipware are exhibited here *(see p74)*.

5 Barbara Hepworth Museum and Sculpture Garden
View sculptures exhibited in Hepworth's former St Ives studio and in her beautiful walled garden *(see p30)*.

6 St Ives Society of Artists Gallery
This private gallery shows rotating exhibitions by local artists *(see p31)*.

7 Broomhill Sculpture Gardens
This gallery and sculpture garden showcases a fantastic collection of contemporary works *(see p118)*.

8 Falmouth Art Gallery
A strong, eclectic collection of over 2,000 works by artists with links to Cornwall *(see pp18–19)*.

9 Penlee House
The best place to see paintings by artists' colony the Newlyn School, with a permanent collection *(see p33)*.

10 Exeter Phoenix
Exeter's main arts centre includes three galleries hosting local and contemporary art shows *(see p69)*.

🔟 Churches, Abbeys and Cathedrals

Stained glass, St Neot's church

incorporates the 600-year-old parish church of St Mary's. Highlights of the interior include Jacobean tombs and Victorian stained glass.

1 St Neot
MAP E3 ▪ St Neot
▪ www.stneot.church

Located in one of Bodmin Moor's prettiest villages, this 15th-century church contains stained-glass windows depicting Noah's Ark and St Neot himself. The church-yard boasts what is claimed to be Cornwall's finest ornamental cross.

2 Truro Cathedral
MAP C5 ▪ St Mary's St, Truro
▪ 01872 276782

Rising over Truro, this Neo-Gothic monument was the first Anglican cathedral constructed in England after St Paul's in London. Built between 1880 and 1910, it

3 St Nonna
MAP E3 ▪ Altarnun
▪ Open 10am–4pm daily

Known as the "cathedral of the moors", this 15th-century church on Bodmin Moor is famous for its 79 bench ends carved with saints, clowns and musicians. The Norman font with its fierce faces has been imitated in local churches, and the "vicar of Altarnun" features in Daphne du Maurier's novel *Jamaica Inn*.

4 Exeter Cathedral
Surrounded by the grassy Cathedral Close and crowned by twin Norman towers, Exeter Cathedral is the grandest of Devon and Cornwall's churches. The 14th-century Minstrels' Gallery, the 15th-century Exeter Clock and Chapter House, and carvings on the choir stalls are among the main attractions (see pp24–5).

5 Buckfast Abbey
This complex on the banks of the River Dart was founded in the 11th century, rebuilt as a Cistercian abbey in 1147,

Buckfast Abbey

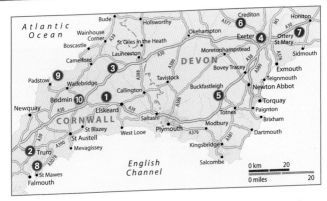

dissolved in 1539 and rebuilt by Benedictine monks between 1907 and 1937. Today, visitors can admire the striking stained-glass windows of the abbey and purchase specialities made by the monks, including tonic wine and beeswax (see p84).

6 Church of the Holy Cross
The grandeur of this red sandstone structure reflects the one-time importance of Crediton, which grew wealthy on wool but is now a mere village. The church is perpendicular in style, with large windows illuminating its rich interior. The east window celebrates Crediton's most famous son, St Boniface (see p81).

7 St Mary
MAP L3 ▪ College Rd, Ottery St Mary ▪ 01404 812062 ▪ www.ottery stmary.org.uk
Set on a hill in poet Samuel Taylor Coleridge's home town, stately St Mary dates from the 13th century. It was enlarged a century later by John de Grandisson, Bishop of Exeter. Noteworthy features include a 14th-century astronomical clock that still works, and the church's exquisite west window, the Apostles Window.

8 St Just-in-Roseland
MAP C5 ▪ St Just-in-Roseland ▪ 01326 270248 ▪ www.stjustand stmawes.org.uk
Situated on the Roseland peninsula, this church, on the shore of a creek,

is surrounded by magnolias and palms. The church dates from 1261, but its battlement tower was added much later, in the 15th century.

9 St Enodoc
This tiny 13th-century church now lies in the middle of a golf course, within sight of the Camel Estuary. The churchyard holds the grave of the poet John Betjeman, who lived for a time in the nearby village of Trebetherick (see p92).

St Enodoc and the Camel Estuary

10 St Petroc's Church
MAP D4 ▪ Bodmin ▪ 01208 77674 ▪ www.stpetrocschurch bodmin.org.uk
Built around 1470, this is the largest parish church in Cornwall and has a typical Cornish wagon roof. Look out for the superb Norman stone font carved with angels, demons and interlacing trees of life.

🔟 Houses

Opulently furnished and panelled interior of Hartland Abbey

1 Hartland Abbey

MAP G2 ■ Hartland, Bideford ■ 01237 441234 ■ Open Apr–Sep: 2–5pm Sun–Thu; grounds open at 11am ■ Adm ■ www.hartland abbey.com

Founded in 1157, this was the last English abbey to be dissolved by Henry VIII (see p38). It has been a private home ever since, and the decor and architecture range from medieval to Victorian-Gothic. Highlights are the vaulted Alhambra Corridor and the Regency library with Gainsborough and Reynolds portraits.

2 Trerice

An architectural gem with ornate fireplaces and elaborate ceilings, this small Elizabethan manor has a good collection of English furniture, clocks and examples of needlework. The highlight is the barrel ceiling of its Great Chamber. Tudor costume days are very popular with visitors (see p92).

Trerice carriage clock

3 Pencarrow

MAP D3 ■ Bodmin ■ 01208 841369 ■ Open Apr–Sep: 11am–5pm Sun–Thu (last tour at 3pm; gardens open until 5:30pm) ■ Adm ■ www. pencarrow.co.uk

This elegant 18th-century mansion is noted for its porcelain and paintings, including portraits by Joshua Reynolds (see p49). The extensive formal and wooded gardens are home to England's first Victorian rock garden.

4 Lanhydrock

This 17th-century palace was rebuilt in the High Victorian style after

Atlantic Ocean

Bideford ① A361
Great Torrington ⑨
Bude Holsworthy Tiverton
A377
Okehampton
Launceston Exeter
Padstow ⑦ Tavistock DEVON
Newquay Bodmin ③ Liskeard ⑧ ⑤ Newton Abbot
② ④ Saltash Torquay
St Ives Redruth CORNWALL A38
Penzance Truro St Austell Plymouth ⑩ Dartmouth
Falmouth Kingsbridge
⑥ Helston

English Channel

0 km   25
0 miles   25

a fire in 1881, but the North Wing containing the Jacobean Long Gallery and the gatehouse survived. The building is filled with the accoutrements of a 19th-century mansion, including elaborate kitchens *(see pp12–13)*.

5 Buckland Abbey

Founded as a Cistercian abbey in 1278, Buckland was disbanded in the Dissolution of the Monasteries, converted into a private home by the distinguished mariner Richard Grenville and subsequently acquired by Francis Drake in 1580. Drake's seafaring exploits are related here and visitors can also admire the Great Barn, which is bigger than the house itself *(see p80)*.

6 St Michael's Mount

This rocky island was linked with Normandy's Mont-St-Michel until 1424 and later became a fortified private home. The best-preserved parts are the Chevy Chase Room, the 14th-century church and the Lady Chapel, later converted into a drawing room. The Blue Drawing Room is embellished in Rococo style with Wedgwood blue furnishings *(see pp32–3)*.

Pretty exterior of Prideaux Place

7 Prideaux Place

This fine manor house has been occupied since 1592 by the Prideaux family. It holds numerous treasures, including loot from the Spanish Armada and the country's oldest cast-iron cannon. The expansive grounds include a classical temple, a deer park, a grotto and a 9th-century Celtic cross *(see p34)*.

Tapestry, Cotehele House

8 Cotehele House

Hidden in the byways of the Tamar Valley, this Tudor palace is a must for all fans of needlework, with the bedrooms adorned in heavy tapestries – the absence of electric lights has helped to preserve them. The house also has four-poster beds and finely crafted furniture. It is best to visit on a sunny day *(see p97)*.

9 Knightshayes Court

MAP K3 ■ Bolham, Tiverton ■ 01884 254665 ■ House: Open Mar–Oct: 11am–5pm daily; Nov–Feb: 11am–4pm daily; (gardens open 10am daily) ■ Adm ■ www.nationaltrust.org.uk

The original designer of this Victorian country pile was the flamboyant architect William Burges. When costs began to rocket, Burges was fired, but enough of his elaborate Gothic-style interiors remain in the library, vaulted hall and the arched red drawing room.

10 Saltram

MAP H5 ■ Plympton ■ 01752 333500 ■ Open Mar–Oct: 11am–4:30pm daily; Nov–Feb: 11am–3:30pm daily ■ Adm ■ www.nationaltrust.org.uk

This majestic 18th-century mansion is set in parkland, outside Plymouth. Its grand exterior is matched by the stately rooms inside (including the Robert Adam saloon) each decorated with a dazzling array of art.

🔟 Castles

Gatehouse of Berry Pomeroy Castle

1 Berry Pomeroy Castle
MAP K5 ■ Totnes ■ 01803 866618 ■ Open Apr–Sep: 10am–6pm daily; Oct: 10am–4pm daily; Nov–Mar: 10am–4pm Sat & Sun ■ Adm ■ www.english-heritage.org.uk

This romantic ruin on the edge of a wooded ravine is reputed to be haunted. Built by the Pomeroy family in the 15th century, the castle was abandoned 200 years later. Ever since, there have been reported sightings of the ghosts of the "White Lady" and the "Blue Lady".

2 Restormel Castle
Still belonging to the Duchy of Cornwall, this perfectly circular Norman castle occupies a spur overlooking the River Fowey. In medieval terms, it was a luxury residence, with unusual facilities including running water that was piped up under pressure from a natural spring. It is now a ruin, but it is still possible to walk right around the castle walls (see p98).

3 Pendennis Castle
The most westerly of the artillery forts built under Henry VIII, Pendennis and its twin St Mawes were built to safeguard the port of Falmouth, the "key to Cornwall". The castle's ramparts and bastions were erected in around 1600 and the gun batteries were added during the Napoleonic wars (see p19).

4 Caerhays Castle
John Nash – architect of Buckingham Palace – designed this fantasy-Gothic structure in 1810. Visitors can tour the castle, but the real showpiece is the garden, with its magnolias and rhododendrons. The adjacent curve of beach is also an excellent place to visit (see p98).

5 Castle Drogo
This 20th-century fortress in the Teign Valley was designed to resemble a medieval stronghold by architect Edwin Lutyens, who was asked to create a replica of the castles of yore. Austere granite walls and a warren of stone corridors give the castle a spartan feel. You can play croquet here in summer (see p17).

6 St Mawes Castle
The most elaborately decorated of Henry VIII's coastal fortresses, this castle follows a clover-leaf design, with round

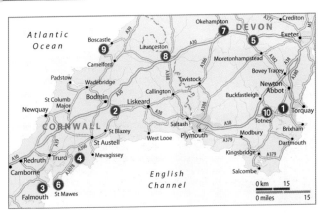

walls that were intended to deflect enemy fire. However, the castle was never tested in war – it surrendered to Parliamentarian forces in 1646 without putting up a fight (see p39). Visitors can tour the gun rooms, governor's quarters, barracks, oubliette and kitchen (see p94).

7 Okehampton Castle

This Norman castle on a spur above the River Okement is a dramatic sight, dominated by the remains of its keep. The fortress, once owned by the Courtenay family – later earls of Devon – was mainly used as a hunting lodge (see p16).

8 Launceston Castle

MAP F3 ■ Launceston ■ 01566 772365 ■ Open Apr–Sep: 10am–6pm daily; Oct: 10am–5pm daily ■ Adm ■ www.english-heritage.org.uk

A motte-and-bailey castle built shortly after the Norman Conquest, Launceston became the power centre from which the Earls of Cornwall

Dramatic St Mawes castle

kept control of their vast estates. Prince Charles was proclaimed Duke of Cornwall here in 1973, receiving two greyhounds as part of his feudal dues.

Ruins of Tintagel Castle

9 Tintagel Castle

Set on a promontory above the turbulent Atlantic, the forlorn ruins of Tintagel resemble a fairy-tale castle. Said to be the birthplace of the mythical King Arthur, the castle was in fact a Norman stronghold (see p89).

10 Totnes Castle

MAP K5 ■ Totnes ■ 01803 864406 ■ Open Apr–Sep: 10am–6pm daily; Oct: 10am–5pm daily; Nov: 10am–4pm Sat & Sun ■ Adm ■ www. english-heritage.org.uk

Towering above the centre of Totnes, this classic Norman construction was erected after the Conquest to donimate the Saxon town. The stone keep was added 300 years later.

🔟 Writers

Portrait of D H Lawrence

1 D H Lawrence

D H Lawrence spent the years 1915–17 in the remote village of Zennor with his wife, Frieda. He loved the "high shaggy moor hills, and big sweep of lovely sea", but was forced to leave in the face of hostility. His life in Cornwall inspired Helen Dunmore's prize-winning novel, *Zennor in Darkness* (1993).

2 Henry Williamson

The novelist and naturalist set his classic animal tale *Tarka the Otter* in the lush countryside of North Devon. The book has been the inspiration for the Tarka Trail (see p74), a recreational route around the Taw and Torridge rivers.

3 Charles Causley

Along with John Betjeman, Causley is one of the best-known 20th-century poets associated with Cornwall. He was born and raised in Launceston, returning to live there in 1946. His work drew on hymns and ballads, and described Cornish life and local legends.

4 Michael Morpurgo

The Isles of Scilly – where children's writer Michael Morpurgo has spent many holidays writing on the island of Bryher – has inspired many of his novels, including *Why the Whales Came*, *The Wreck of the Zanzibar* and *Listen to the Moon*.

5 Winston Graham

All 12 of Graham's *Poldark* novels, written between 1945 and 2002, were set mainly around Perranporth, but also took in other parts of Cornwall, including Mousehole and Lanhydrock. The books have enjoyed great success as TV adaptations.

6 R D Blackmore

Although he wrote a number of novels, Blackmore is best remembered today for his swashbuckling romance *Lorna Doone* (1869), set on Exmoor in the 17th century. Fans can visit the novel's locations, including the Valley of the Rocks outside Lynmouth.

R D Blackmore's *Lorna Doone*

7 Sir Arthur Conan Doyle

Dartmoor inspired Conan Doyle's *The Hound of the Baskervilles*, based on a number of local legends about super-natural black dogs that inhabited remote parts of the moor (see p17).

Sir Arthur Conan Doyle

Agatha Christie at Greenway

⑧ Agatha Christie

Born in Torquay, the "Mistress of Murder" spent much of her life in South Devon, particularly at Greenway (see p84), a grand mansion overlooking the River Dart. The settings of her country-house whodunnits give a strong flavour of the area. Torquay Museum has a good exhibition devoted to her.

⑨ Kenneth Grahame

Kenneth Grahame regularly took breaks in Cornwall, and began writing The Wind in the Willows as letters to his young son while staying at the Greenbank Hotel in Falmouth. A boat trip along the River Fowey inspired the opening scene, where Ratty and Mole make a trip along the river for a picnic.

⑩ Daphne du Maurier

Having spent many childhood holidays in Cornwall, du Maurier eventually settled outside Fowey. Drawn to Cornwall's secluded creeks and the wild romance of the moors, she set some of her famous novels here – including Rebecca and Jamaica Inn. An annual arts festival in Fowey celebrates her work (see p68).

TOP 10 ARTISTS IN CORNWALL AND DEVON

1 Joshua Reynolds
Raised near Plymouth, Reynolds was one of the foremost portrait artists of the 18th century.

2 Elizabeth Forbes
Born in Canada in 1859, this successful Newlyn painter was best-known for her portrayal of women and children.

3 Stanhope Forbes
Husband of Elizabeth Forbes, the Irish-born artist was a leading figure of the Newlyn School (see p41).

4 Norman Garstin
This artist's most famous work, The Rain It Raineth Everyday (1889), is on display in Penlee House, Penzance.

5 Alfred Wallis
A simple fisherman, who was "discovered" by the St Ives artists, Wallis is known for his naive style.

6 Bernard Leach
A higly influential potter, Leach was based for a long time in St Ives.

7 Barbara Hepworth
The St Ives studio of this sculptor is now a gallery displaying her works.

8 Ben Nicholson
Hepworth's husband from 1938 to 1951, Nicholson exerted great influence with his austere, abstract paintings.

9 Terry Frost
One of Britain's most prominent abstract painters, Terry Frost was based mainly in St Ives and Newlyn.

10 Patrick Heron
This artist's highly coloured abstract works are typified by his giant stained-glass window in the Tate St Ives.

Houses in St Ives (c.1940), by Wallis

🔟 Gardens

Sleeping Mud Maid in ancient woodlands, Lost Gardens of Heligan

① Lost Gardens of Heligan

There is an air of mystery about this "lost garden". First planted in the late 18th century, the garden was neglected to the point of decay until it was rediscovered by Tim Smit, the guiding light behind the Eden Project *(see pp14–15)*. Smit restored the garden while preserving its wild, tangled character. The site includes walled flower gardens and a sub-tropical "Jungle" valley *(see p96)*.

Trengwainton Gardens in bloom

② Trengwainton Gardens

MAP A5 ■ Madron, Penzance
■ 01736 363148 ■ Open mid-Feb–
Oct: 10:30am–5pm Sun–Thu ■ Adm
■ www.nationaltrust.org.uk

Visitors to this diverse garden can enjoy an abundance of exotic trees, shrubs, sheltered walled gardens and a woodland area. In spring, the blooming azaleas, camellias and rhododendrons add to the colourful display. Picnic by the stream or enjoy the views from the terrace.

③ Bicton Park

This extensive estate has formal parterres of bedding plants and a renowned collection of trees, including a giant Grecian Fir. There is an elegant Palm House, dating from the 1820s, while the Tropical House features the Bicton orchid. A woodland railway provides scenic rides through the landscaped park *(see p82)*.

④ Trelissick Garden

Sheltered by woodlands, this Cornish garden features rhododendrons, magnolias and acers. Bordering the River Fal, the site affords views across the Carrick Roads Estuary *(see p19)*.

⑤ Tresco Abbey Garden

First planted in 1834, these Isles of Scilly gardens have been carefully nurtured by five generations of the same family. The region's climate, the mildest in the UK, has allowed the cultivation of exotic plants from around the southern hemisphere. The Tresco Abbey ruins form an evocative backdrop *(see p27)*.

6 Rosemoor
MAP H2 ■ Great Torrington
■ 01805 624067 ■ Open Apr–Sep:
10am–6pm daily; Oct–Mar: 10am–
5pm daily ■ Adm ■ www.rhs.org.uk

In North Devon's Torridge Valley,
Rosemoor provides year-round
interest, with snowdrops in winter,
rhododendrons in spring, flower
borders in summer and fiery hues
in autumn. The most spectacular
displays, however, are 2,000 roses
with more than 200 cultivars. Woodland walks provide further interest.

Glendurgan garden's maze

7 Lanhydrock
Surrounding this grand manor
house are a number of horticultural
spectacles, including a unique
yew-hedged herbaceous garden,
at its best in summer. Other highlights are magnolias from Sikkim,
Tibet and southern China, as well
as hybrid rhododendrons and
geraniums (see pp12–13).

8 Trebah
This subtropical
garden has a selection
of 100-year-old tree
ferns and water gardens
with koi carp. Plants
grown here have been intro-
duced from around the
world, including gunnera
(giant rhubarb) from Brazil
and Australasian tree ferns.
Rhododendrons and hydrangeas
lead to a private beach on the
River Helford (see pp18–19).

**Flower from
Lanhydrock**

9 Glendurgan
This wooded valley garden
on the banks of the Helford has
walled areas and herbaceous
planting with brilliant colour and
foliage. The spring-flowering
magnolias and camellias
are especially impressive.
Children will enjoy the baffling
laurel maze dating from
1833 and the Giant's Stride
rope swing (see p104).

10 Mount Edgcumbe
Located on the Rame
Peninsula outside Plymouth,
Mount Edgcumbe has Italian,
French and American formal
gardens and is home to the national
camellia collection, which flowers
from January. The grounds include
follies and a deer park (see p66).

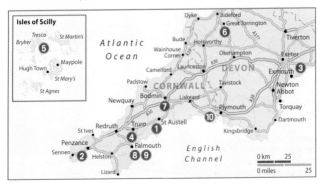

⭐10 Beaches

Sheltered bay at Blackpool Sands

1 Blackpool Sands
Backed by lovely woods and meadows, this family-friendly beach is an enticing sight as it swings into view on the road from Dartmouth. Its sheltered location, clear water and fine sand make it one of South Devon's best swimming spots. The renowned Venus Café provides refreshments.

2 Par Beach, Isles of Scilly
MAP B4

Majestic, bare and wild, the beaches on St Martin's are considered to be the best on the Isles of Scilly. Par Beach, on the island's southern shore, is probably the most impressive – a long, empty strand looking out onto rocks that make up the Eastern Isles. If you are planning to take a dip, be prepared for chilly water.

3 Whitesand Bay
MAP A5

This expanse of fine sand close to Land's End is a favourite with surfers and families alike. It has a good beachside café and at Sennen Cove, the more popular southern end of the beach, is the Old Success Inn (see p116). Surfing equipment can be hired and surfing courses are available.

4 Porthcurno
One of the finest bays on the Penwith Peninsula, Porthcurno, with its wedge of white sand mixed with tiny shells, is squeezed between granite cliffs. The rock-hewn Minack Theatre is located to one side and there is a museum of telegraphy at the back of the beach. There are some good pubs and cafés to be found here, too (see pp28–9).

5 Watergate Bay
MAP C4

North of Newquay, this arc of golden sand has a wild appeal. It is home to the Extreme Academy, which offers kitesurfing, landboarding and other pursuits for the adventurous. Behind the bay are Jamie Oliver's restaurant, Fifteen, and the more casual Beach

Watergate Bay

Hut (see p93), both with splendid views. Watergate is not very sheltered, so make sure you carry some windbreakers.

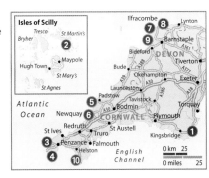

6 Fistral Bay
MAP C4

Surf enthusiasts flock to this beach, a venue for surfing competitions. A surf centre supplies equipment for hire. Most of the sand is covered by water at high tide, and strong currents mean that children especially need to be careful. Lifeguards are present throughout the summer. You can watch all the action (without getting wet) from the outdoor tables at many of the restaurants and cafés.

Surfer riding the waves at Fistral Bay

7 Woolacombe Bay

Surfers come from far and wide to one of the West Country's most famous surfing beaches. The beach is popular with families and there is a warren of dunes behind for exploring. Crowds gather at the northern end, but more space can be found at the quieter southern end. The small resort of Woolacombe has shops and cafés (see p73).

8 Tunnels Beaches, Ilfracombe
MAP H1 ■ Bath Place, Ilfracombe ■ 01271 879882 ■ Open May–Sep: 10am–6pm daily; Jul–Aug: 10am–7pm; Oct: 10am–5pm Tue–Sun ■ Adm ■ www.tunnelsbeaches.co.uk

These private beaches are named after the tunnels that have provided access to them since 1823, when the swimming was segregated. There is a tidal bathing pool and top-class rock-pooling with on-duty lifeguards. One beach is often closed for weddings.

9 Croyde Bay
MAP H1

Sandwiched between the extensive west-facing Saunton Sands and Woolacombe, this compact bay has fine sand. There are camp sites nearby and the village has pubs and bars that fill up in the evenings.

10 Kynance Cove
MAP B6

This is one of the best options on the Lizard Peninsula, where beaches are few and far between. The 10-minute walk from the car park is well worth the trudge for the beach's fine white sands, rocky spires and surrounding grassy areas. Swimming is limited by the tides, but other attractions here include caves and cliffs with serpentine seams of sand.

Kynance Cove, Lizard Peninsula

TOP 10 Walks

Walking the Two Moors Way

1 Two Moors Way/ Coast-to-Coast Walk

MAP J1–K1

The Two Moors Way, which links Exmoor and Dartmoor, can be extended at its southern end between Ivybridge and Wembury to make a 188-km (117-mile) coast-to-coast hike. The most dramatic scenery is on Dartmoor, though Lynmouth at the northern end makes a striking end point.

2 Camel Trail

The Camel River flows through some of Cornwall's most beautiful landscapes, from the edge of Bodmin Moor to the sea at Padstow. A 27-km (17-mile) bike and walking trail follows a disused railway line (much admired by John Betjeman) through wooded valleys to the wide-open tidal mudflats of the Camel Estuary (see p89).

3 Tarka Trail

Inspired by Henry Williamson's animal tale *Tarka the Otter*, this figure-of-eight route centres on Barnstaple and takes in coastal and inland areas of North Devon. If you include the section covered by the Tarka Line between Eggesford and Barnstaple, the route is 288 km (180 miles) (see p74).

4 Coast and Clay Trail

MAP D4–C5

This 75–km (45-mile) network of shorter interlinked paths around Truro, St Austell and the Roseland Peninsula, is designed to give a taste of Cornish history – from gardens and fishing villages to the china clay industry and the Eden Project.

5 Saints Way

Cornwall's coast-to-coast trail covers about 48 km (30 miles) between Padstow and Fowey. There is no evidence that the whole route was used in the Middle Ages, but parts of it were certainly travelled by pilgrims en route to shrines, holy wells and chapels (see p35).

6 Dart Valley Trail

MAP J5

Experience the Dart Valley on this 26-km (16-mile) walk, which swoops high above or runs alongside the River Dart. Half of it is a circuit, involving two ferry crossings, and the other half follows the river to Totnes.

Hiker on the South West Coast Path

7 Dartmoor Way
MAP J4

This circular 153-km (95-mile) route crosses some of Dartmoor's most thrilling terrain, including rugged moorland, wooded valleys and disused railway tracks. Much of the trail skirts the edge of the moor, but it also takes in Princetown in the centre of Dartmoor.

 8 East Devon Way
MAP L4

Also known as the Foxglove Way, this undulating inland trail follows footpaths, bridleways and lanes between Exmouth and Uplyme, north of Lyme Regis over the Dorset border. It is 61 km (38 miles) long.

 9 St Michael's Way
MAP B5

Weaving between Lelant, near St Ives, and Marazion, this 19.5-km (12.5-mile) trail was once used by pilgrims and travellers to avoid the treacherous waters at Land's End.

 10 South West Coast Path

At 1,014 km (630 miles) in length, this is England's longest National Trail, used by anyone who walks for any distance along the Devon and Cornwall seaboard. Starting in Minehead in Somerset, and winding along the coasts of Devon, Cornwall and finally Dorset, this scenic trail is predominantly hilly and often dramatic (see p111).

TOP 10 WATER SPORTS

Gig Racing at Salcombe

1 Stand-Up Paddleboarding
SUP is hugely popular, with boards, tuition and guided paddles offered on many beaches across the region.

2 Sea Kayaking
This is a fantastic way to explore sheltered coastlines and the Isles of Scilly, as well as tidal rivers and creeks.

3 Canoeing
Enjoy the rivers of Dartmoor and the waterways of Cornwall on a canoe trip.

4 Coasteering
This increasingly popular pursuit involves negotiating rocky coasts using a variety of means.

5 Sailing
Salcombe, Dartmouth, Falmouth and Fowey offer a great range of facilities for sailors of all levels.

6 Surfing
Some of Britain's top surfing beaches can be found in the West Country, with annual competitions at Newquay.

7 Windsurfing
The region's bays and inlets are ideal for windsurfers, with rental equipment available at many places.

8 Diving
The wrecks and reefs off the coast of Devon and Cornwall attract diving enthusiasts from far and wide.

9 Gig Racing
Ex-pilot boats are raced off the coastal villages of West Cornwall in summer, most famously in the Isles of Scilly.

10 Sea Safaris
Take to the seas on one of these organized whale-, seal- and shark-watching excursions during summer.

Train Rides

Steam train on the privately run Bodmin and Wenford Railway

1 Bodmin and Wenford Railway
MAP D4 ▪ 01208 73555
▪ www.bodminrailway.co.uk

The steam or diesel engines of this private standard-gauge line provide an excellent way to explore the countryside around Bodmin. The terminus at Bodmin Parkway is linked by a 3-km (2-mile) path to Lanhydrock (see pp12–13). There is direct access to the Camel Trail from Boscarne Junction and to Cardinham Woods from Colesloggett Halt.

2 Looe Valley Line
MAP E4 ▪ 08457 484950

The Cornish fishing port of Looe is linked to Liskeard by this branch line dating from 1860. The route runs beside the river through the heavily wooded Looe Valley.

3 Atlantic Coast Line
MAP C4–D4 ▪ 08457 484950

This 33-km (21-mile) coast-to-coast line runs from the English Channel at Par Station to Newquay on the Atlantic, passing through the lunar landscape of china clay country.

4 Exeter to Newton Abbot
MAP K4 ▪ 08457 484950

Between Exeter and Newton Abbot, the main line runs beside two estuaries, the Exe and the Teign, offering delightful vistas over serene mudflats populated by wading birds.

5 Tarka Line
MAP H1–H3 ▪ 08457 484950

Named after Tarka the Otter, which was largely set in the area, this 65-km (39-mile) line, centred on Barnstaple, weaves through Devon's rural heartland. After Crediton, it sticks close to the River Taw, passing through woodland inhabited by woodpeckers and buzzards.

6 Tamar Valley Line
MAP F4 ▪ 01752 584777

The highlight of this branch line is the Calstock Viaduct between Devon and Cornwall. A "rail ale trail" is available for those wanting to drink en route.

Calstock Viaduct, Tamar Valley Line

7 South Devon Railway

From a station outside Totnes, the steam trains of the South Devon Railway depart several times daily between April and October (and some dates in winter), for a scenic ride to Buckfastleigh, on the edge of Dartmoor. There is a stop at Staverton, with access to a path beside the River Dart (see p84).

8 Launceston Steam Railway

MAP F3 ▪ 01566 775665
▪ www.launcestonsr.co.uk

These narrow-gauge Victorian steam engines run for 4 km (2.5 miles) between Launceston and Newmills. At Launceston Station visitors can see restoration projects as well as vintage cars and motor-bikes at the Transport and Engineering Museum.

Launceston Steam Railway

9 Paignton and Dartmouth Steam Railway

MAP K5 ▪ 01803 555872
▪ www.dartmouthrailriver.co.uk

This heritage line runs from Paignton Station around the Tor Bay coast, then follows the River Dart to Kingswear. A round trip ticket includes a river cruise from Dartmouth to Totnes and the coach ride back to Paignton.

10 St Erth to St Ives

MAP B5 ▪ 08457 484950

This picturesque branch line is the best way to reach St Ives (see pp30–31). It edges along the Hayle Estuary before winding around the beaches of St Ives Bay, ending up steps away from Porthminster Beach.

TOP 10 BEAUTY SPOTS

Golitha Falls, Bodmin Moor

1 Lydford Gorge, Dartmoor
This lovely spot has riverside walks, a whirlpool and a waterfall (see p17).

2 Hartland Point
Cliffs and crags flank this rocky promontory, which offers spectacular views of Lundy Island (see p76).

3 Roseland Peninsula
One of the region's most photogenic and least spoiled spots, with two waterside churches (see p96).

4 Valley of the Rocks, Exmoor
This dry valley has striking rock formations and coastal views (see p76).

5 Golitha Falls, Bodmin Moor
MAP E3
A series of waterfall cascades gush through oak and beech woodland.

6 Lizard Point
MAP C6
A wild, rocky promontory at England's southern tip, with invigorating walks to beaches and a famous lighthouse.

7 Watersmeet, Exmoor
A canopy of oaks covers this beautiful confluence of the East Lyn and Hoar Oak rivers. Perfect for walks (see p76).

8 Cape Cornwall, Penwith Peninsula
MAP A5
The ocean pounds against this craggy headland, which is overlooked by an abandoned chimney stack.

9 Dartmeet, Dartmoor
The West and East Dart rivers merge here, near a clapper bridge and close to a nature reserve (see p17).

10 Hell Bay, Isles of Scilly
On the island of Bryher, this dramatic, stunning bay bears the full brunt of Atlantic storms (see p26).

TOP 10 Children's Attractions

Thrill ride, Flambards

1 Flambards

MAP B5 ■ Helston ■ 01326 573404 ■ Open Apr–Oct: 10am–5pm daily (last entry at 3pm) ■ Adm ■ www.flambards.co.uk

Attractions here include a re-created Victorian village, where 50 shops and cottages are on show, and an exhibition of Britain in the Blitz. Thrills are provided by the Hornet Roller Coaster, Skyswinger and the Log Flume, while the Aviation Experience offers interactive fun.

2 Kents Cavern

MAP K5 ■ Ilsham Rd, Torquay ■ 01803 215136 ■ Open daily; check website for tour times ■ Adm ■ www.kents-cavern.co.uk

Stone Age living is brought to life in one of the country's most significant prehistoric sites, with guided tours of the caves, treasure hunts, foraging trails and cave painting. There are also spooky evening ghost tours and a series of special seasonal events.

3 Newquay Zoo

Cornwall's only zoo, set in lakeside gardens, is home to lions, lynxes, meerkats and tortoises. Fun activities for kids include exploring the Tarzan Trail and getting lost in the Dragon Maze (see p90).

4 National Seal Sanctuary

In this rescue centre, watch recovered and orphaned seals and pups frolic in outdoor pools. Sometimes there are dolphins and turtles, and the centre also cares for otters, ponies, goats and penguins. Feeding times and talks are popular daily events (see p104).

National Seal Sanctuary

5 Babbacombe Model Village

MAP K5 ■ Hampton Ave, Babbacombe, Torquay ■ 01803 315315 ■ Opening times vary ■ Adm ■ www.model-village.co.uk

This miniature world features working railways, landscaped gardens, a celebrity mansion, a naturist beach and a 4D theatre, plus a few indoor displays. After dusk, 10,000 bulbs light up the streets, homes and gardens.

Babbacombe Model Village

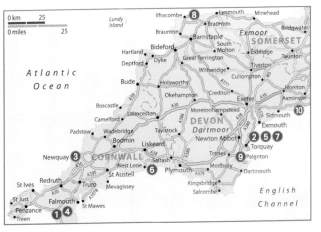

(6) The Monkey Sanctuary
MAP E4 ■ St Martin's, Looe
■ 01503 262532 ■ Open Apr–Sep:
11am–4:30pm Sun–Thu ■ Adm
■ www.monkeysanctuary.org

This lovely charitable sanctuary overlooking Looe Bay promotes the welfare of South American woolly and capuchin monkeys and Barbary macaques. A colony of lesser horseshoe bats housed here can be observed via cameras and infrared lights. The Treetop Café serves delicious vegetarian food.

(7) Living Coasts
Focusing on the conservation of coastal and marine life, this aquatic zoo features the flora and fauna that can be found along Britain's coasts. Living exhibits include avocets, puffins and cormorants, though the Penguin Beach and Fur Seal Cove are the perennial favourites (see p81).

(8) Watermouth Castle
MAP H1 ■ Berrynarbor,
Ilfracombe ■ 01271 867474
■ Opening times vary ■ Adm
■ www.watermouthcastle.com

This Victorian folly castle and adventure park includes a model railway, crazy golf and toboggan run. The castle itself displays suits of armour and a 1950s organ on which life-size figures play instruments.

(9) Paignton Zoo
Gorillas and gibbons can be seen here, and many of the animals can be viewed from the Jungle Express railway, popular with children. Close-up experiences with rhinos, meerkats and giraffes are available (see p82).

Beer Heights Light Railway, Pecorama

(10) Pecorama
MAP M4 ■ Underleys, Beer,
Seaton ■ 01297 21542 ■ Open Apr–
Oct: 10am–5pm daily ■ Adm ■ www.
pecorama.co.uk

The star attraction of this park, home to the model railway manufacturers, is a ride on the 7.25-inch-gauge Beer Heights Light Railway – a one-third scale steam train, running along a mile of track with coastal views.

TOP 10 Places to Eat

Gidleigh Park's main building amid beautiful grounds

1 Gidleigh Park

A two-Michelin-starred restaurant headed by Michael Wignall, with a contemporary, informal approach to fine dining. The menu is constantly evolving, with unique dishes accompanied by vegetables and herbs grown in the kitchen garden. It boasts a prestigious wine cellar with 13,000 bottles from around the world (see p85).

2 The Masons Arms

This fantastic Michelin-starred pub-restaurant on the edge of Exmoor is owned by chef Mark Dodson, who trained with Michel Roux. Locally sourced food is taken to new levels, and the atmosphere is relaxed. Dine outside in good weather (see p77).

Dining room at The Masons Arms

3 Kota Restaurant

New Zealand chef Jude Kereama, who is half-Maori, half-Malay Chinese, brings an Asian twist to meticulously sourced Cornish produce in his award-winning restaurant above the harbour at Porthleven, although there are plenty of European influences too (see p107).

4 The Seafood Restaurant

Rick Stein's flagship fish and seafood restaurant, founded in 1975, is buzzy and unpretentious, featuring many of the dishes familiar from his books and TV programmes. The sticky, spicy Singapore crab – impossible to eat without using your fingers – is incredible. If you don't have a booking, there is a seafood bar in the middle of the restaurant where you can sit and watch chefs assembling platters of oysters, langoustines and sashimi (see p93).

5 The Elephant Restaurant and Brasserie

The informal atmosphere of the Elephant suits its Torquay location, but this is no ordinary seaside eatery. Chef Simon Hulstone has created a Michelin-starred restaurant, with sustainable fish, and meat and vegetables from his farm (see p85).

6 The Coach House

A glass window allows diners to watch the chefs at work in this restaurant from Devon's culinary star, Michelin award-winning chef Michael Caines. The menu is strictly seasonal and relies on local produce *(see p77)*.

7 Nathan Outlaw

Trained with Rick Stein, two-Michelin-starred chef Nathan Outlaw has two restaurants and a pub in Cornwall. The flagship is Nathan Outlaw at Port Isaac, which serves just one set tasting menu *(see p93)*.

8 Driftwood Restaurant

A relaxed and understated Michelin-starred hotel-restaurant on the Roseland Peninsula. Meat, fish and vegetables are all locally sourced, and over-sophistication is shunned in favour of bringing out the very best in the prime ingredients *(see p99)*.

Sea views at Driftwood Restaurant

9 The Hidden Hut

Porthcurnick Beach is home to a tiny beach café whose feast nights (two or three each month, March–September) sell out instantly. The formula is simple: there's one dish and you bring your own alcohol. It's fun, relaxed and perfect for families *(see p99)*.

10 Crab Shack

This converted cowshed at Hell Bay is hung with nets and nautical paraphernalia and the tables are upcycled doors from the old abbey on Tresco. The menu couldn't be simpler – crabs, mussels or scallops, plus chips, salad and wine *(see p106)*.

TOP 10 PLACES FOR CREAM TEAS

Exterior of New Yard

1 Otterton Mill
MAP L4 ▪ Otterton, Budleigh Salterton ▪ 01395 567041
Fine organic scones are baked and served at this ancient mill.

2 Falmouth Hotel
MAP C5 ▪ Castle Beach, Falmouth ▪ 01326 312671
Nibble scones on the hotel terrace.

3 New Yard, Trelowarren
MAP B5 ▪ Mawgan, Helston ▪ 01326 221595
Cream teas are served daily during summer in this estate's pretty stableyard.

4 Dwelling House
Scones and an excellent choice of cakes in an eclectic tearoom *(see p99)*.

5 Weavers Cottage Tea Shoppe
MAP K5 ▪ Cockington, Torquay ▪ 01803 605407
Thatched cottage serving tea-time treats.

6 Southern Cross
MAP L4 ▪ Newton Poppleford, nr Sidmouth ▪ 01395 568439
A walled garden here provides the perfect setting for afternoon tea.

7 Clock Tower Café
MAP L4 ▪ Connaught Gardens, Sidmouth ▪ 01395 515319
Enjoy the sea-views while indulging in delicious home-made cakes.

8 Watersmeet House
A lovely spot for tea and cakes *(see p77)*.

9 Polpeor Café
MAP C6 ▪ The Lizard ▪ 01326 290939
England's southernmost café has impressive seascapes and tasty scones.

10 Rectory Farm and Tea Rooms
MAP E2 ▪ Crosstown, Morwenstow, near Bude ▪ 01288 331251
Feast on cakes and scones beside an open fire in a 13th-century farmhouse.

For a key to restaurant price ranges see p77

📖 Pubs

The Masons Arms, Branscombe

1 The Masons Arms
MAP M4 ▪ Branscombe
▪ 01297 680300

Located 10 minutes from the beach, this East Devon inn dispenses great locally brewed bitter and serves top-notch food, including local mussels and crab. You can sit outside under the thatched table umbrellas, and rooms are also available upstairs.

2 The Sloop Inn
MAP B5 ▪ St Ives ▪ 01736 796584

One of Cornwall's oldest pubs, with beams, benches and nooks, the Sloop is a popular St Ives haunt right on the harbour. It offers a fine range of real ales and decent pub fare. Punters spill out onto the cobbled harbourside in summer.

3 Ship Inn, Mousehole
This excellent inn stands directly above the harbour in a tiny fishing village. The Tinners and Tribute ales and fish pie are worth sampling. If you miss out on a seat with harbour views, sit in the tiny patio garden upstairs. Accommodation is also available (see p106).

4 Turk's Head
MAP B5 ▪ Chapel St, Penzance
▪ 01736 363093

Said to be Penzance's oldest pub, the Turk's Head dates from 1233 and has a maze of low-ceilinged rooms, a beer garden and a smugglers' tunnel.

5 Blue Anchor Inn
Dating back to the 15th century, this lovely Helston pub, which was originally a monks' rest house, has been brewing its own beer, Spingo Ale, for 600 years (see p106).

6 Tinners Arms
MAP A5 ▪ Zennor ▪ 01736 796927

This historic pub, which dates from 1271, is where D H Lawrence (see p48) stayed when he came to live in Zennor. There's a log fire, and live music is played most Thursdays. Children are also welcome.

The Sloop

7 Prospect Inn, Exeter
MAP P3 ■ The Quay, Exeter
■ 01392 273152

Right on the waterfront, family-friendly Prospect Inn has tables outside on the quay – a good spot for watching the sun set during the summer months. Well-cooked meals are served with a good range of local beers and ciders.

8 Blisland Inn
MAP E3 ■ Blisland ■ 01208 850739

A traditional country pub on Bodmin Moor, the Blisland Inn has Toby jugs hanging from wooden beams and walls festooned with photographs. A wide variety of real ales and tasty pub food is available.

Interior of the Blisland Inn

9 Warren House Inn
MAP J4 ■ 4 km (2 miles) NE of Postbridge, Dartmoor ■ 01822 880208

The third-highest pub in England stands in solitary splendour on Dartmoor. It is a welcome sight to walkers, with two hearths – one that has reputedly been kept burning since 1845 – and good food.

10 Bridge Inn
MAP K4 ■ Bridge Hill, Topsham ■ 01392 873862

The pink-walled, 16th-century Bridge Inn, with its real ales and traditional trappings, is one of Devon's best pubs. It is reputedly the only pub to have been graced by the Queen in an official capacity, when she visited the region in 1998.

TOP 10 LOCAL BREWERIES

1 Skinners
This Truro-based brewery features ales named after Cornish locations and folk heroes, such as Betty Stogs.

2 St Austell
This is Cornwall's major brewer, whose traditional cask ales include the legendary HSD and Tribute.

3 Sharp's
The Cornish producer of fine beers such as Doom Bar, Wolf Rock, Coaster, Atlantic Sea Fury and Orchard.

4 Otter
A Honiton-based brewery which produces five regular beers and one winter ale available throughout Devon.

5 O'Hanlon's
Located in Devon, this small, specialist brewery produces some award-winning cask and bottled beers.

6 Country Life
Bideford-based producer of ales such as Old Appledore, the light-coloured Golden Pig, and Country Bumpkin.

7 Spingo Ales
These famous brews are available only in Helston's Blue Anchor, in four distinctive varieties from 4.5 per cent to 6.5 per cent ABV.

8 Driftwood Spars Brewery
Award-winning microbrews from the Driftwood Spars brewpub at St Agnes.

9 Ales of Scilly
The Scilly-based producer of Firebrand and Scuppered bitters, with some additional seasonal beers.

10 Harbour Brewing Company
A progressive Cornish microbrewery offering a range of innovative beers.

St Austell beer mats

🔟 Shopping

1 Totnes Elizabethan Market

MAP K5 ▪ Civic Square, Totnes ▪ 01803 863714 ▪ Open May–Sep

Every Tuesday morning throughout summer, local traders dress up in Tudor costumes for the Elizabethan market, which runs alongside an all-day crafts market.

Branch of the Seasalt clothing chain

2 Bickleigh Mill

MAP K3 ▪ Bickleigh, Tiverton ▪ 01884 855419 ▪ www.bickleigh mill.com

A working 18th-century watermill is the venue for this retail centre, which sells jewellery, ceramics and soaps, seasonal gifts and toys.

3 Tavistock Pannier Market

MAP H4 ▪ Tavistock ▪ 01822 611003

Tavistock's indoor market offers antiques and collectables (Tuesdays), crafts (Wednesdays and Thursdays), local produce (Fridays), popular collectables (first Saturday of the month) and mixed markets (third and fourth Saturday of the month).

4 Seasalt

MAP C5 ▪ Sale Shop: Unit 17, Kernick Business Park, Annear Rd, Penryn ▪ 01326 379451

This is the sale outlet of the nationwide Cornwall-based company, which creates women's clothes inspired by the Cornish coast and landscape – including signature raincoats. There are around a dozen branches located across Devon and Cornwall.

5 Darts Farm

MAP K4 ▪ Topsham, Exeter ▪ 01392 878200 ▪ www.darts farm.co.uk

From its launch as a farm shop, Darts has evolved into an entire shopping hub based around the concept of fresh, locally sourced food. On site you can find a food hall, butchers, deli, fish shed and cider works, and also a restaurant and health and beauty treatments.

6 Cream of Cornwall

MAP C5 ▪ 51 Church St, Falmouth ▪ 01326 317253

This is the flagship store of a small Cornish interiors chain, which is best-known for its monochrome printed china. It also sells popular textiles and lampshades with designs featuring fish, lobsters and jellyfish.

Tavistock Pannier Market

7 Cornwall Crafts Association

Trelowarren branch: MAP B5; Mawgan-in-Meneage, Helston; 01326 221567 ■ **Trelissick Gardens branch: MAP C5; Feock, Truro: 01872 864514** ■ **www.cornwallcrafts.co.uk**

A range of top quality Cornish arts and crafts are exhibited and sold at two locations. The goods are inspired by contemporary trends.

8 Duchy of Cornwall Nursery

MAP E4 ■ **Cott Road, Lostwithiel** ■ **01208 872668** ■ **www.duchyof cornwallnursery.co.uk**

One of the largest nurseries in the South West England, this place is an inspiration for gardeners, offering a range of shrubs, ornamental and fruit trees, climbers and conservatory plants. Among its specialities are various conifers, fuchsias, bamboos and camellias.

Duchy of Cornwall Nursery

9 Barnstaple Pannier Market

A lively market is held daily until around 4pm in this purpose-built hall dating from 1855. Come for books, clothing, household goods, local produce, crafts and antiques (see p75).

10 Devon Guild of Craftsmen

MAP K4 ■ **Riverside Mill, Bovey Tracey** ■ **01626 832223**

This consortium sells some of the region's best contemporary crafts, including ceramics, textiles, jewellery and furniture. Its base on the edge of Dartmoor holds regular exhibitions.

TOP 10 THINGS TO BUY

Creamy Cornish fudge

1 Local Art
Buy local art at small galleries, which are to Devon and Cornwall what antique shops are to the Cotswolds.

2 Serpentine
A speciality of the Lizard Peninsula, this greenish rock is used to make a variety of local ornaments.

3 Fudge
Creamy and delicious flavoured fudge is available in almost every gift shop throughout the region.

4 Ice Cream
Most resorts have at least one shop selling quality ice cream in a range of contemporary flavours.

5 Local Wine and Gin
West Country wines are among the country's finest, while historic Plymouth Gin is internationally famous.

6 Fishermen's Apparel
Fishing smocks, caps and woolly jumpers are widely available and make great mementos and souvenirs.

7 Crafts
Hand-crafted woodwork, jewellery, silverware and glassware are among the South West's specialities.

8 Fresh Seafood
Experience the thrill of buying seafood directly from the harbour. It can usually be iced and packaged if you have a long trip back home.

9 Surf Gear
All the major surf gear brands are represented at outlets in the surfing centres of Devon and Cornwall.

10 Pottery
Some of the country's most renowned potters are based in the South West and exhibit their wares in the region.

🔟 Cornwall and Devon for Free

1 Falmouth Art Gallery

This family-friendly gallery has a collection of 2,000 artworks, ranging from Pre-Raphaelite paintings to contemporary prints, photographs and children's illustrations. It also has the UK's largest public collection of automata. There are workshops for families and a constantly changing programme of exhibitions (see p19).

Mount Edgcumbe formal gardens

2 Mount Edgcumbe

Although there is a fee to enter the house, access to the grounds – with more than 324 ha (800 acres) of beautiful parkland, formal gardens and the National Camellia Collection – is free. There are walks along the seashore among rare trees and plants, as well as a good chance of glimpsing wild fallow deer (see p98).

3 Marconi Centre, Poldhu

MAP B6 ▪ Near Mullion ▪ 01326 241656 ▪ Opening hours vary ▪ donation requested ▪ www.marconi-centre-poldhu.org.uk

This small heritage centre was built on the site from which Guglielmo Marconi transmitted the first ever transatlantic radio message to Signal

Merrivale Prehistoric Settlement

Hill, St John's, Newfoundland on 12 December 1901. A short video presentation and information boards relate the fascinating story.

4 Cornish Camels

MAP B5 ▪ Rosuick Organic Farm, St Martin, Helston ▪ www.cornishcamels.com ▪ 01326 231302

Organic livestock farm on the Lizard Peninsula, set in its own beautiful valley. Visitors are free to follow paths around the farm, and there are peacocks as well as a herd of camels.

5 Roskilly's Ice Cream Farm

MAP C6 ▪ Tregellast Barton Farm, St Keverne ▪ 01326 280479 ▪ www.roskillys.co.uk

Roskilly's Cornish ice cream is sold throughout the county. At this organic farm you can watch the cows being milked as well as enjoy the ice cream. There are also marked trails through the wild meadows, and cows, goats, pigs, sheep, turkeys, geese, quails and chickens to be seen.

6 Merrivale Prehistoric Settlement, Dartmoor

MAP H4 ▪ On B3357, W of Princetown ▪ www.english-heritage.org.uk

The remains of a Bronze Age village of round houses and several ritual structures can be found on Dartmoor, including three stone rows, a stone circle, standing stones and a number of burial mounds. These monuments were built between 2500 and 1000 BC, but one of the most distinctive stones is medieval – a huge round of granite once used for crushing cider apples.

Buckfast Abbey and gardens

7 Buckfast Abbey

The abbey and its grounds, including an aromatic lavender garden and a physic garden where medicinal herbs are cultivated, is home to a thriving community of Benedictine monks. There is also a shop selling crafts and produce made by monks and nuns from all over Europe (see p84).

8 Geocaching in Devon
www.geocaching.com

Devon is a perfect location for geocaching – treasure-hunting via smartphone – with more than 25,000 geocaches scattered along its vast network of paths and cycle tracks. Geocachers use GPS to hide containers and then post clues to help seekers. The app is free to download from the website.

9 Shoalstone Pool, Brixham

MAP K5 ■ Berry Head Rd ■ Open May–Sep ■ www.shoalstonepool.com

This Art Deco lido was built in 1926, with a seawater swimming pool dating from 1896, and is maintained by volunteers and the local council. There is a fee for parking, and for those who decide to hire a beach hut or lounger, but use of the pool is free.

10 Heartlands, Pool

MAP B5 ■ Robinson's Shaft, Dudnance Lane ■ 01209 722320

A free leisure and cultural centre created around a disused tin mine in Cornwall's UNESCO-designated mining country. There are interactive exhibitions on the history of mining, plus gardens and a good café.

TOP 10 BUDGET TIPS

1 National Trust Membership
Membership not only gives free access to the region's many NT properties, but also free parking at various beauty spots.

2 Beach Picnics
Look out for artisan breads, local cheeses and farm-grown fresh produce sold from farm shops, and enjoy your feast with a spectacular view.

3 Multiday Tickets
Entry tickets at many attractions are valid for 7 days and some – including for the Eden Project and the National Aquarium – are valid for one year.

4 Wine and Cider Tastings
Look out for free tastings at vineyards and cider farms around the counties.

5 Bus Passes
In Devon, the weekly Megarider Gold ticket gives access to all routes run by Stagecoach South West.

6 Self-Catering Websites
Stay on a camp site or look out for self-catering accommodation using an owner-led website (see p115).

7 Take the Sleeper
Save time – and a night's stay – by travelling on the Night Riviera train from London Paddington to Cornwall.

8 Book Ahead
Book in advance online for the Eden Project and save 10 per cent.

9 Discount Vouchers
Look out for vouchers giving discounted entry to sights or special deals in cafés and restaurants. They can be found at most regional tourist offices.

10 Stay Inland
Accommodation inland and off the beaten track in Cornwall can be good value, while still within easy driving distance of the coast.

The Eden Project

🔟 Festivals

1 Obby Oss, Padstow

MAP D3 ■ 1 May (or 2 May if date falls on Sun)

Pagan fertility rites and local traditions unite in this May Day spectacle. The main character, the Obby Oss, garbed in a black costume draped around a 2-m- (6-ft-) wide hoop, is accompanied by a "Teazer" with music, drumming and the May Song.

Sidmouth Folk Week performers

2 Helston's Flora Day

MAP B5 ■ 8 May (or previous Sat if date falls on Sun or Mon)

This uniquely Cornish extravaganza involves a stately procession of top-hatted people in frocks performing the "Furry Dance" through the streets of Helston. Flowers and sprigs of sycamore feature too.

3 Fowey Festival of Arts and Literature

MAP E4 ■ Mid-May ■ www.fowey festival.com

Run by the Daphne du Maurier Society, this 8-day literary festival celebrates the author, who lived in Fowey, and features music, drama, walks, workshops and daily talks.

4 Golowan Festival, Penzance

MAP B5 ■ Late Jun ■ www.golowan festival.org

This week-long arts and dance festival features processions, circus acts, buskers and a mock mayoral election. The Golowan Band provides music, while flaming torches and fireworks add to the spectacle.

5 Sidmouth Folk Week

MAP L4 ■ Early Aug ■ www.sidmouthfolkweek.co.uk

Folk music, Northumbrian pipes and Morris dancers feature at a seaside festival in one of Devon's most elegant towns. Even non-folk fans succumb to the event's upbeat charm, with buskers lining the Esplanade and pubs jammed with carousers. Accommodation and concert tickets sell out quickly.

6 St Ives September Festival

MAP B5 ■ Mid-Sep ■ www.stivesseptemberfestival.co.uk

The arts have long had a strong presence in St Ives and this two-week jamboree brings them together with exhibitions, drama and poetry readings. Music ranges from cello recitals to tribute pop acts and African beats, with most performances held at the Guildhall and the Western Hotel. There are also talks and comedy performances.

Golowan Festival procession

Dartmouth Royal Regatta

The three-day regatta features rowing races and yachting displays. It became "royal" after an unscheduled visit by Queen Victoria in 1856. There's a distinct martial flavour with military bands and an air display by the RAF.

 Oyster Festival, Falmouth

MAP C5 ▪ Mid-Oct ▪ www.falmouth oysterfestival.co.uk

This four-day event pays homage to Cornish seafood. There's music from the local brass band, oyster-shucking competitions, cookery demonstrations and boat races.

Tar barrelling at Ottery St Mary

 Tar Barrelling, Ottery St Mary

MAP L3 ▪ 5 Nov (or previous Sat if date falls on Sun)

Every Bonfire Night, tar-soaked barrels are set alight and hoisted around town and there are races for men, women and children. The evening culminates in fireworks and a huge bonfire beside the River Otter.

 Tom Bawcock's Eve, Mousehole

MAP A5 ▪ 23 Dec

A procession and fireworks celebrate the fisherman who saved the village from starvation by going to sea in a storm and landing a huge catch of pilchards, which were served up in stargazy pie – the Cornish pie with the fish heads poking through the top.

TOP 10 LIVE MUSIC AND THEATRE VENUES

1 Exeter Phoenix
MAP P2 ▪ Gandy St ▪ 01392 66 7080 ▪ www.exeterphoenix.org.uk
Exeter's premier arts centre.

2 Eden Project
This is Cornwall's best outdoor music venue in summer (see pp14–15).

3 The Poly, Falmouth
MAP C5 ▪ 24 Church St ▪ 01326 319461 ▪ www.thepoly.org
Year-round venue for exhibitions, art cinema, theatre and concerts.

4 Hall for Cornwall, Truro
MAP C5 ▪ Back Quay ▪ 01872 262466 ▪ www.hallforcornwall.co.uk
Drama and music are staged here.

5 Exeter Northcott
MAP N1 ▪ Stocker Rd ▪ 01392 726363 ▪ www.exeternorthcott.co.uk
Exeter's principal theatrical venue.

6 Minack Theatre
This amphitheatre hosts a range of productions in summer (see pp28–9).

7 Acorn Arts Centre, Penzance
MAP B5 ▪ Parade St ▪ 01736 363545 ▪ www.theacornpenzance.com
This former church is now a playhouse.

8 Calstock Arts Centre, Calstock
MAP F3 ▪ The Old Chapel ▪ 01822 833183 ▪ www.calstockarts.org
Calstock's arts centre hosts a wide range of live music, theatre and comedy.

9 Barbican Theatre, Plymouth
MAP Q6 ▪ Castle St ▪ 01752 267131 ▪ www.barbicantheatre.co.uk
A theatre specializing in new drama.

10 Theatre Royal, Plymouth
MAP P5 ▪ Royal Parade ▪ 01752 267222 ▪ www.theatreroyal.com
Mainstream shows are held in the main theatre, while the Drum Theatre hosts cutting-edge performances.

Exeter Phoenix performance

Cornwall and Devon Area by Area

Hawthorn tree and granite outcrop
at sunrise on Dartmoor

TOP 10 North Devon

Between the austere heights of Exmoor and the rocky pinnacles of Hartland Point, North Devon crams in a rich landscape. Two of the region's top nature reserves, Northam Burrows and Braunton Burrows, and some of the best beaches, such as Woolacombe Bay, Saunton Sands and Westward Ho!, are located on this stretch of coast. The main towns are Barnstaple, Ilfracombe and Bideford, but the true treasures are the coastal villages of Appledore and Clovelly. Inland, the Tarka Trail is ideal for cycling or walking, while out at sea, Lundy Island is home to puffins and seals.

Lighthouse on Lundy Island

1 Lundy Island
MAP G1 ■ Tourist information: 01271 863636 ■ www.nationaltrust. org.uk/lundyisland or www.landmark trust.org.uk/lundyisland
This remote 5-km- (3-mile-) long sliver of land is located north of Hartland Point and is name after the puffins that live here ("lunde" is medieval Norse for puffin). There are options for overnight stays, including a lighthouse and a radio room. Day trips sail from Ifracombe and Bideford in summer.

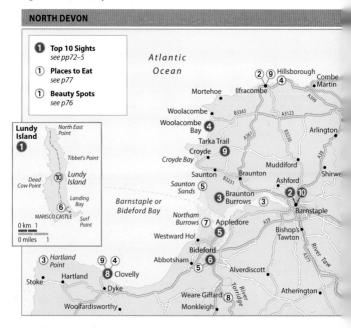

NORTH DEVON

1 Top 10 Sights
see pp72–5

1 Places to Eat
see p77

1 Beauty Spots
see p76

2 Museum of Barnstaple and North Devon

MAP H2 ■ The Square, Barnstaple ■ 01271 346747 ■ Open Apr–Oct: 10am–5pm Mon–Sat; Nov–Mar: 10am–4pm Mon–Sat

This museum includes features on the area's wildlife and a gallery devoted to *Tarka the Otter (see p74)*. You can walk through a model Wellington bomber and view charming timepieces and beautifully crafted glassware. The Barum Ware – pottery for which the area is renowned – is superb.

3 Braunton Burrows

MAP H2

The core of a UNESCO-designated biosphere, this wild and windblown area constitutes the largest sand-dune system in the UK. The dunes are stabilized by marram grass and other plants. Nearly 500 species of vascular plants and a variety of invertebrates live here. Meandering paths traverse the area, which can be reached on the Tarka Trail and the South West Coast Path *(see pp54–5)*.

Bodyboarders at Woolacombe Bay

4 Woolacombe Bay

MAP H1

Surfers know this impressive arc of sand as one of the country's top sites for riding the waves, but non-surfers will find plenty of space here, especially at the more sheltered southern end, Putsborough. Surf gear can be rented at shops and stalls above the beach, where there are also a handful of cafés and bars.

5 Appledore

MAP H2 ■ Maritime Museum: 01237 422064; open Apr–Oct: 10:30am–5pm daily; adm; www.northdevonmaritimemuseum.co.uk

A stately air hangs over this village of Georgian houses at the edge of the Torridge Estuary. Behind the seafront, narrow lanes with shops and pubs lead uphill to the Maritime Museum with its collection of nautical items. For the best estuary views, tasty seafood and a pint, head for one of the two pubs on Irsha Street.

Bude Street in Appledore

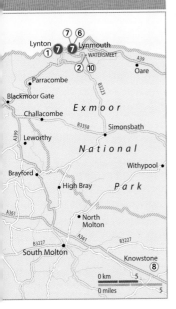

⑥ Burton Art Gallery and Museum

MAP H2 ▪ Kingsley Rd, Bideford
▪ 01237 471455 ▪ Open 10am–4pm
Mon–Sat (Aug: to 5pm), 11am–4pm
Sun ▪ www.burtonartgallery.co.uk

The "little white town" of Bideford, rich with historical associations and home of the Elizabethan mariner Sir Richard Grenville, houses the Burton Art Gallery and Museum. The gallery boasts an absorbing collection of art and artifacts, including watercolours, model ships and replicas of the famed local slipware. The museum is located in Victoria Park, where cannons taken from the Spanish Armada are exhibited.

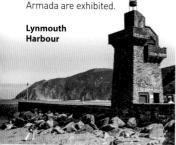

Lynmouth Harbour

⑦ Lynton and Lynmouth

MAP J1

These villages on the Exmoor coast, linked by a water-powered funicular, have drawn visitors since the 1800s when the poet Shelley spent his honeymoon here. Nestled among hills, the villages are a haven of tranquillity, though it was not always peaceful here. Lynmouth, by the sea, was devastated by a flash flood in 1952; the Glen Lyn Gorge, through which the torrent raged, holds an exhibition in memory of the event.

⑧ Clovelly

MAP G2 ▪ Tourist information:
01237 431781; www.clovelly.co.uk

This picturesque settlement clings to a steep cliff and plunges down to a small harbour. The town is privately owned and there is an absence of cars, except for a Land Rover service

Clovelly's pretty harbourfront

for visitors who find the steep main street unmanageable. Some of the cottages are open to the public, including a museum dedicated to Charles Kingsley, author of *The Water Babies*, who lived here as a child.

⑨ Tarka Trail

MAP H1–H3

Henry Williamson's classic animal fable *Tarka the Otter* was set around his native North Devon. The otter's epic journeys are traced in this 288-km (180-mile) trail, which describes a figure of eight centred on the town of Barnstaple and incorporating sections of the South West Coast Path and Tarka Line railway. Over 50 km (31 miles) of the trail, between Braunton and Meeth, can be cycled. Other sections take in the scenic Taw Valley and Williamson's home village of Georgeham.

TARKA THE OTTER

North Devon's Tarka Line, Tarka Trail and Tarka Country all refer to *Tarka the Otter*, written by Henry Williamson. The book narrates the adventures of a young otter amid the beautiful landscape of North Devon – "the country of the two rivers". The book has retained its place as a classic animal tale, and was made into a film in 1979, narrated by Peter Ustinov.

Atlantic Ocean

Ilfracombe

Lynton and Lynmouth

Woolacombe

Croyde

Broomhill Art Hotel

Appledore

Barnstaple

Hartland Abbey

Clovelly

Burton Art Gallery and Museum

▶ **MORNING**

Begin your tour in the sister villages of **Lynton and Lynmouth** at the foot of Exmoor. The upper village, Lynton, is connected by an ingenious cliff railway to Lynmouth. From here it is a short drive to **Ilfracombe**, a cheerfully traditional resort with a bustling harbour. On the coast south of Ilfracombe, **Woolacombe** (see p73) and **Croyde** (see p53) beaches invite a stopover. Though very different – Croyde is a sheltered inlet while Woolacombe is a long, curving bay – both are good for families as well as water sports enthusiasts. You can indulge in a beachside picnic lunch or drive inland to lunch at the restaurant in the **Broomhill Art Hotel** (see p118), where the sculpture will prove absorbing.

AFTERNOON

In the afternoon, make a stop at **Barnstaple**, home to the lively **Pannier Market** as well as the **Museum of Barnstaple and North Devon** (see p73). Or you could instead call in at Bideford for a visit to the **Burton Art Gallery and Museum**, which hosts regular exhibitions. Up at the mouth of the estuary, **Appledore** (see p73) has another museum you can explore, but a stroll along the riverside is equally enjoyable. Proceed west along Bideford Bay to **Clovelly**, an enchanting, well-preserved village, and stop here for a cup of tea. If time allows, continue west to **Hartland Abbey** (see p44), a majestic mansion with lovely grounds sweeping down to the sea.

⑩ Barnstaple Pannier Market

MAP H2 ▪ Butchers Row, Barnstaple ▪ 01271 379084 ▪ Open Mon–Sat ▪ barnstaplepanniermarket.co.uk

This covered market in the town centre is the most famous of Devon's "pannier markets" – so called because traders originally brought their wares in baskets or panniers. Antiques, crafts, local produce, household items and clothes are all on sale here. Alongside is Butchers Row, which once held butchers' shops and is now home to a variety of stores selling clothes, antiques, household items and gifts.

Barnstaple Pannier Market

See map on pp72–3

Beauty Spots

① Valley of the Rocks
MAP J1

West of Lynton, this steep heathland is dominated by rugged rock formations. Herds of wild goats still roam free as they have done here for centuries.

Watersmeet's woodland gorge

② Watersmeet
MAP J1

In a deep wooded gorge, Hoar Oak Water joins with the East Lyn River on its way down to the sea. Shady riverside walks branch out from here.

③ Hartland Point
MAP G2

On Devon's northwestern tip, overlooked by a solitary lighthouse, this remote, storm-battered headland has dramatic views of slate cliffs, jagged black rocks and swirling sea.

④ Hillsborough
MAP H1

Outside Ilfracombe, the summit of this 136-m (447-ft) hill is one of the few places in the country where you can see the sun rise and set over the sea.

⑤ Saunton Sands
MAP H2

The first view of this 6-km (4-mile) westward-facing strand is breath-taking, with ranks of Atlantic rollers advancing in stately fashion. This spot is a favourite among surfers.

⑥ Lynmouth
The East and West Lyn rivers flow placidly into the sea at this cliff-sheltered Exmoor village. The Glen Lyn Gorge has woodland walks and waterfalls (see p74).

⑦ Northam Burrows
MAP H2

Located next to Westward Ho!, this expanse of grasslands, salt marsh and sand dunes offers wonderful views across the Taw/Torridge Estuary. The broad beach in front attracts surfers and sail-boarders.

⑧ Weare Giffard
MAP H2

This graceful village in the wooded Torridge Valley boasts a 15th-century manor house and a weathered pub. It is accessible from the Tarka Trail.

⑨ Clovelly
One of the loveliest Devon villages, with neat cottages and a miniature harbour (see p74).

⑩ Lundy Island
This remote outpost where the Atlantic meets the Bristol Channel is either utterly tranquil or in complete uproar, depending on the sea (see p72).

Hillsborough

Places to Eat

PRICE CATEGORIES
For a three-course meal for one with
half a bottle of wine, including taxes and
extra charges.

£ under £35 ■ ££ £35–£55 ■ £££ over £55

(1) The Coach House
MAP H2 ■ Kentisbury Grange,
Barnstaple ■ 01271 882295 ■ £££
A stylish country hotel on the edge
of Exmoor hosts this restaurant by
Devon-born chef Michael Caines.

(2) The Olive Room
MAP H1 ■ 56 Fore St, Ilfracombe
■ 01271 867831 ■ Closed Mon, Thu L &
Sun ■ £££
The chef, Thomas Carr, serves creative
and contemporary dishes using the
freshest of local produce. There's an
excellent selection of wines.

(3) Fremington Quay Café
MAP H2 ■ Fremington Quay,
Barnstaple ■ 01271 268720 ■ £
This café is a perfect stop on the Tarka
Trail from Barnstaple to Bideford. It
serves cakes, cream teas and lunch.

(4) Red Lion
MAP G2 ■ Clovelly ■ 01237
431237 ■ ££
A harbourside inn with great views,
where you can eat locally caught fish
and game from the Clovelly Estate.
There are rooms upstairs *(see p116)*.

(5) Mariners
MAP F1 ■ 4 Cooper St, Bideford
■ 01237 476447 ■ Closed Sun; Oct–
May: Mon & Tue ■ ££
A relaxed, contemporary restaurant,
a short walk from the quay, serving
food prepared using local ingredients.

(6) Marisco Tavern
MAP G1 ■ Lundy Island
■ 01237 431831 ■ £
Lundy's sole pub serves island
specialities using Soay lamb and
venison from Sika deer. Highland
cattle can be found near the tavern.

(7) Rising Sun
MAP J1 ■ Harbourside,
Lynmouth ■ 01598 753223 ■ ££
Contemporary cuisine – featuring
seafood – is served in a 14th-century
inn that claims to have once accommodated poet Percy Shelley.

(8) The Masons Arms
MAP J2 ■ Knowstone, South
Molton ■ 01398 341231 ■ Closed Mon,
Sun (except first Sun of the month)
■ £££
This welcoming Michelin-starred
restaurant is set in a thatched
13th-century pub on the edge of
Exmoor, with excellent food, and
outside dining in good weather.

The Masons Arms

(9) The Quay
MAP H1 ■ 11 The Quay,
Ilfracombe ■ 01271 868090 ■ ££
This chic harbourside restaurant has
cracking views and features artwork
by co-owner Damien Hirst, along
with a Modern European menu.

(10) Watersmeet House
MAP J1 ■ Watersmeet Rd,
Lynmouth ■ 01598 753348 ■ Open
daytime, closed Nov–mid-Mar ■ £
At a famous Exmoor beauty spot,
this Victorian fishing lodge, run
by the National Trust, is now an
inviting tearoom and garden.

See map on pp72–3

TOP 10 South Devon

A genteel aura pervades much of South Devon. Verdant meadows are interspersed with cob-and-thatch villages, and rivers drift serenely through wooded valleys dotted with tidy cottages. Crumbling red cliffs rear above beaches, while in the forbidding expanse of Dartmoor, lonely tors punctuate slopes of bracken and gorse, and isolated communities are huddled around centuries-old churches. A world away from these rural scenes are the cathedral cities of Exeter and Plymouth, the region's historic power centres, both with a scattering of medieval and Elizabethan remains to explore.

Living Coasts penguin

SOUTH DEVON

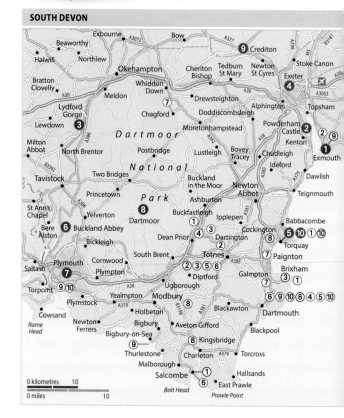

① A La Ronde

MAP L4 ▪ Summer Lane, Exmouth ▪ 01395 265514 ▪ Open mid-Feb–Oct: 11am–5pm daily ▪ Adm ▪ www.nationaltrust.org.uk

When cousins Jane and Mary Parminter returned from their European travels in 1790, they brought with them trunkloads of souvenirs and a unique vision. They built this 16-sided house and filled it with mementos and quirky creations. These range from seaweed and sand concoctions to a frieze of game-bird and chicken feathers, and a shell-covered gallery.

Façade of Powderham Castle

② Powderham Castle

MAP K4 ▪ Kenton ▪ 01626 890243 ▪ Open Apr–Oct: 11am–4:30pm Sun–Fri ▪ Adm ▪ www.powderham.co.uk

Surrounded by a deer park, this stately pile is the long-time seat of the earls of Devon. Tours take in the ornate music room, the majestic dining room, lavish bedrooms and the Victorian kitchen. There are kids' activity trails in the grounds.

③ Lydford Gorge

On the edge of Dartmoor, the River Lyd gushes noisily through this oak-wooded ravine, home to the spectacular Devil's Cauldron whirlpool and the White Lady Waterfall that plummets 28 m (90 ft). There are walks along the river and a winding upper path but sturdy boots are required, and children must be supervised. Access may be difficult for those with impaired mobility *(see pp16–17)*.

White Lady Waterfall, Lydford Gorge

English Channel

4 Exeter

Devon's capital is a relaxed city with a historic core that includes the region's oldest cathedral and a treasure trove of a museum. Among other attractions is a network of underground passages and an old quayside. The city has an active cultural life, with year-round festivals and events, and a good selection of restaurants (see pp22–5).

The Children's Holiday (1865) by William Holman Hunt, Torre Abbey

5 Torre Abbey

MAP K5 ▪ King's Drive, Torquay ▪ 01803 293593 ▪ Open 10am–5pm Tue–Sun ▪ Adm ▪ www.torre-abbey. org.uk

One of Devon's best museums is housed in a mansion converted from abbey buildings after the Dissolution of the Monasteries in 1539 (see p38). Its strong 19th-century art collection includes works by Holman Hunt and Burne-Jones. The grounds hold medieval ruins and a tithe barn.

DEVON'S RESORTS

Devon's south coast benefited from the 19th-century development and extension of Britain's railway network. With the influx of visitors, villas and *cottage ornés* (thatched, rustic dwellings) sprang up in fashionable towns such as Torquay, Exmouth and Sidmouth.

6 Buckland Abbey

MAP H5 ▪ Yelverton ▪ 01822 853607 ▪ Open mid-Feb–Oct: 11am–5pm daily; times vary in winter ▪ Adm ▪ www.nationaltrust.org.uk

The former home of Elizabethan mariners Richard Grenville and Francis Drake, this handsome manor house occupies beautiful grounds in the Tavy Valley. Visitors can look round the monastic Great Barn, Elizabethan Garden and the main Abbey, where galleries feature interactive displays. Exhibits include Drake's Drum which, according to legend, will sound again when England is in danger to summon Drake from his grave.

7 Plymouth

MAP H5

This historic city contains remnants of its Elizabethan glory days, notably in the harbourside Barbican quarter. Other attractions include the National Marine Aquarium (see p40) and the Plymouth Gin Distillery (see p82). Don't miss the magnificent sea views from Plymouth Hoe, a high, grassy esplanade above the harbour.

8 Dartmoor

In a region dominated by the sea, Dartmoor is a windy wasteland where semi-wild ponies roam. Prehistoric remains are scattered across the moor, while on its edges lie the market towns of Okehampton and Tavistock. Dartmoor offers great opportunities for walking, canoeing and wildlife watching (see pp16–17).

Ponies on Dartmoor

Church of the Holy Cross

⑨ Church of the Holy Cross
MAP K3 ■ Church St, Crediton
■ 01363 773226

This red sandstone structure from
the 15th century is one of Devon's
grandest churches. Its east window
features the key points in the life
of the great missionary St Boniface,
who was born in AD 680. The extensive and intricate memorial of 1911,
occupying the east wall of the nave,
is dedicated to Sir Redvers Buller.
He was awarded the Victoria Cross
in the 1879 Zulu War.

⑩ Living Coasts
MAP K5 ■ Beacon
Quay, Torquay ■ 01803 202470
■ Open 10am–dusk daily ■ Adm
■ www.livingcoasts.org.uk

Here, reconstructed beaches,
cliff faces and an estuary show
off the diversity of coastal wildlife
around the world. An aviary hosts
cormorants, penguins and puffins;
there are also South American fur
seals to watch.

A DRIVING TOUR IN SOUTH DEVON

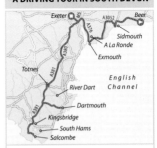

▶ **MORNING**

Start close to the Dorset border
at the fishing village of **Beer** (see
p83), associated with the exploits
of the infamous smuggler Jack
Rattenbury. You can grab a crab
sandwich on the beach. Follow
the A3052 west to **Sidmouth** (see p83),
whose seafront and esplanade
are perfect for a stroll. The town
is studded with well-preserved
villas from the Regency period.
The museum here includes a
lovely display of lace. Indulge in
a hearty seaside lunch by the
waterfront before leaving town.

AFTERNOON

Continuing west, just outside
Exmouth (see p83) off the A376,
stop to admire **A La Ronde** (see
p79), a remarkable 16-sided folly
constructed by cousins Jane and
Mary Parminter. Go north to the
M5, then take the A380 and A381
south to **Totnes** (see p83). Despite
its hippy vibe, the town retains
much of its Elizabethan character
and has a Norman castle and a
14th-century church. The town's
tearooms are a good place to stop
for some refreshments. From
Totnes, drive or take a river cruise
along the River Dart to the sailing
resort of **Dartmouth** (see p83),
also filled with reminders of the
Elizabethan era. From Totnes or
Dartmouth, it is an easy excursion
to the South Hams, an area of
sleepy villages and peaceful
views. Unless you are based in
Totnes or Dartmouth, either stay
over in Kingsbridge or **Salcombe**
(see p83), or head back up the
A381 to **Exeter** (see pp22–5).

See map on pp78–9

The Best of the Rest

A hiker looking out across Berry Head

① Berry Head, Torbay
MAP K5

This coastal headland and nature reserve is home to guillemots and the endangered Greater Horseshoe Bat.

② Fairlynch Museum
MAP L4 ▪ 27 Fore St, Budleigh Salterton ▪ 01395 442666 ▪ Open Apr–Oct: 2–4:30pm Tue–Sun & bank hols

This 19th-century *cottage orné* holds a collection of lace, costumes and toys.

③ Beer Quarry Caves
MAP M4 ▪ Quarry Lane, Beer ▪ 01297 680282 ▪ Open Apr–Sep: 10:30am–4:30pm, Oct: 10:30am–3:30pm ▪ Adm ▪ www.beerquarrycaves.co.uk

This limestone quarry, first established by the Romans, supplied stone for Exeter and St Paul's cathedrals.

④ Bicton Park
MAP L4 ▪ East Budleigh, Budleigh Salterton ▪ 01395 568465 ▪ Open from 10am daily, check website for details ▪ Adm ▪ www.bictongardens.co.uk

A horticultural idyll, Bicton includes a 1730s formal garden reputedly inspired by Versailles, and a Palm House from the 1820s.

⑤ Allhallows Museum
MAP L3 ▪ High St, Honiton ▪ 01404 44966 ▪ Open Apr–Oct: Mon–Sat ▪ Adm ▪ www.honitonmuseum.co.uk

Housed in the oldest building in Honiton, this museum displays fine lace.

⑥ Overbeck's Museum
MAP J6 ▪ Sharpitor, Salcombe ▪ 01548 842893 ▪ Open mid-Feb–Oct: 11am–5pm daily ▪ Adm ▪ www.nationaltrust.org.uk

A quirky collection gathered by inventor and scientist Otto Overbeck is housed in this museum.

⑦ Paignton Zoo
MAP K5 ▪ Totnes Rd, Paignton ▪ 01803 697500 ▪ Open 10am–6pm, winter closes 5pm ▪ Adm ▪ www.paigntonzoo.org.uk

This zoo is designed to mimic the natural habitats of the animals that live here.

⑧ Kingsbridge Cookworthy Museum
MAP J6 ▪ 108 Fore St, Kingsbridge ▪ 01548 853235 ▪ Open Apr–Oct: Mon–Sat ▪ Adm

The museum is named after the pioneer of English porcelain made from china clay.

Paignton Zoo rhino

⑨ Burgh Island
MAP J6 ▪ Bigbury-on-Sea

This tiny isle is reached by sea tractor at high tide. Stay overnight at the ritzy Burgh Island Hotel *(see p117)*.

⑩ Plymouth Gin Distillery
MAP P5 ▪ 60 Southside St ▪ 01752 665292 ▪ Open 10:30am–4:30pm Mon–Sat, 11:30am–3:30pm Sun ▪ Adm ▪ www.plymouthdistillery.com

Tours of England's oldest working gin distillery include tastings.

Towns and Villages

1 Salcombe
MAP J6

At the mouth of the placid Kingsbridge Estuary, Devon's southernmost port is a magnet for sailors. Beaches, coastal walks and Overbeck's Museum are all nearby.

2 Totnes
MAP K5

The age of this riverside town is attested by its Norman castle and medieval remains. It is popular with craftworkers and produces some of the country's finest glass and crystal.

3 Brixham
MAP K5

Much of the seafood served in the region's restaurants is landed at this harbour. A magnificent replica of the *Golden Hind*, the vessel in which Francis Drake circumnavigated the globe, is moored here.

4 Budleigh Salterton
MAP L4

John Everett Millais painted his famous *Boyhood of Raleigh* while on this village's pebble beach. The Fairlynch Museum is well worth a visit.

5 Sidmouth
MAP L4

The queen of East Devon resorts, elegant Sidmouth has a long esplanade fronted by a shingle strand. Families prefer the more secluded Jacob's Ladder beach to the west.

Shingle beach, Sidmouth

6 Dartmouth
MAP K6

The Royal Regatta *(see p84)* and the Royal Naval College confirm this port's yachting credentials. Cobbled streets, impressive Tudor buildings and a castle add to its allure.

7 Beer
MAP M4

The village is best-known for fishing, smuggling and Beer stone, a prized building material. A culvert carries a stream along the main street, from where you descend to the beach.

Thatched cottages in Cockington

8 Cockington
MAP K5

There is no denying the rustic appeal of this well-preserved village, a peaceful contrast to the ebullience of neighbouring Torquay.

9 Exmouth
MAP L4

Primarily a family resort, Exmouth becomes quite lively during the summer. The Beacon, an elegant row of Regency houses overlooking the sea, once accommodated the wives of Byron and Nelson.

10 Torquay
MAP K5

Capital of the so-called English Riviera, engaging Torquay, with its palms and fairy lights, smacks unmistakably of the Mediterranean.

See map on pp78–9

Sights Along the River Dart

① Buckfast Abbey
■ MAP J5 ■ Buckfastleigh
■ 01364 645500 ■ Open 9am–6pm
Mon–Sat, noon–6pm Sun ■ www.
buckfast.org.uk
The river flows through the grounds
of this Benedictine house. The monks
here produce a famous tonic wine.

Dartington Hall lawns

② Dartington Hall
■ MAP J5 ■ 01803 847070
■ www.dartington.org
Founded by US heiress Dorothy
Elmhirst, this arts and education
centre hosts various cultural events.

③ Elizabethan Museum
■ MAP K5 ■ 70 Fore St, Totnes
■ 01803 863821 ■ Open Apr–Sep:
10am–4pm Tue–Fri ■ Adm
This museum, in a cloth merchant's
home from 1575, has a room devoted
to Totnes-resident mathematician
Charles Babbage, who built the fore-
runner of the computer.

④ South Devon Railway
■ MAP J5 ■ Station Rd,
Buckfastleigh ■ 01364 644370
■ Open mid-Mar–Oct ■ Adm
■ www.southdevonrailway.co.uk
Travel back in time in a vintage Great
Western Railway coach hauled by a
steam locomotive. The line follows
a scenic route alongside the River Dart
between Totnes and Buckfastleigh.

⑤ Totnes Guildhall
■ MAP K5 ■ 5 Rampart's Walk
■ 01803 862147 ■ Open May–Sep:
11am–3pm Mon–Fri
Built on the ruins of a priory in 1553,
the Guildhall later housed a courtroom
and jail. It displays a table believed to
have been used by Oliver Cromwell.

⑥ Riverlink Cruises
■ MAP K5 ■ 5 Lower St,
Dartmouth ■ 01803 555872 ■ Adm
■ www.dartmouthrailriver.co.uk
The most relaxing way to explore the
Dart is during a 90-minute cruise
between Totnes and Dartmouth.

⑦ Greenway
■ MAP J6 ■ Galmpton ■ 01803
842382 ■ Open Mar–Dec: times vary;
book parking in advance ■ Adm
■ www.nationaltrust.org.uk
Set on the river bank and linked with
Dittisham village by ferry, Agatha
Christie's holiday home, furnished
in 1950s style, is full of her family's
collections of books, china and more.

⑧ South Devon Chilli Farm
■ MAP J6 ■ Loddiswell, near
Kingsbridge ■ 01548 550782
This farm cultivates over 200 types of
chilli, and some can be seen growing
in season. There's a café and a shop.

**⑨ Dartmouth Royal
Regatta**
MAP K5 ■ 01803 834912 (during the
Regatta) ■ late Aug ■ www.dartmouth
regatta.co.uk
Pageantry is the order of the day at
this annual jamboree celebrating
the port's maritime traditions.

⑩ Dartmouth Museum
■ MAP K5 ■ Duke St ■ 01803
832923 ■ Open Apr–Oct: 10am–4pm
Tue–Sat, 1–4pm Sun & Mon; Nov–
Mar: 1–3pm daily ■ Adm ■ www.
dartmouthmuseum.org
A great collection of maritime
models and more is housed in
this former merchant's house.

Places to Eat

1 The Elephant Restaurant and Brasserie

MAP K5 ■ 3 & 4 Beacon Terrace, Torquay ■ 01803 200044 ■ Open Tue–Sat ■ £££

This Michelin-starred restaurant features local fish and seafood, and meat and vegetables raised and grown on the chef's farm (see p60).

2 Lympstone Manor

MAP L4 ■ Courtlands Lane, Exmouth ■ 01395 202040 ■ ■ £££

The latest venture by Exeter-born culinary genius Michael Caines is this boutique country hotel with three restaurants and its own vineyard.

3 Riverford Field Kitchen

MAP J5 ■ Wash Farm, Buckfastleigh ■ 01803 762074 ■ ££

A friendly, organic farm restaurant, serving hearty lunches and dinners at wooden communal tables.

Rockfish's airy dining room

4 Rockfish

MAP K6 ■ 8 South Embankment, Dartmouth ■ 01803 832800 ■ ££

The first branch of chef and writer Mitch Tonks' seafood restaurant is laid-back yet chic. There are other branches in Torquay, Brixham, Exmouth and Plymouth.

5 Café Alf Resco

MAP K5 ■ Lower St, Dartmouth ■ 01803 835880 ■ Breakfast and lunch only ■ No credit cards ■ £

A local favourite, this child-friendly café with a terrace serves pastries, baguettes and lunchtime specials.

PRICE CATEGORIES

For a three-course meal for one with half a bottle of wine, including taxes and extra charges.

£ under £35 ££ £35–£55 £££ over £55

6 The Curator Kitchen

MAP K5 ■ 2 The Plains, Totnes ■ 01803 865570 ■ ££

An Italian osteria where local produce from Totnes and the Marche region of Italy come together with well-chosen wines. The Curator Café below serves wood-roasted coffee.

7 Gidleigh Park

MAP J4 ■ Chagford ■ 01647 432367 ■ £££

Michael Wignall is the latest chef to lead this double Michelin-starred kitchen. His inventive menu combines Far East influences with an excellent selection of meticulously sourced local ingredients (see p60).

8 The Pig at Combe

MAP L3 ■ Gittisham, Honiton ■ 01404 540400 ■ Closed Wed–Sun ■ ££

This is a romantic Elizabethan manor house hotel. It has a restaurant with a kitchen garden, sources its own vegetables and offers outdoor seating.

9 Barbican Kitchen

MAP Q6 ■ 58 Southside St, Plymouth ■ 01752 604448 ■ Closed Sun ■ ££

Set in the historic Plymouth Gin Distillery (see p82), this relaxed brasserie is famed for its Friday fish and chips, using the day's catch fresh from the boats at Looe in Cornwall.

10 Seahorse

MAP K6 ■ 5 South Embankment, Dartmouth ■ 01803 835147 ■ Closed Sun & Mon ■ £££

Mitch Tonks' flagship restaurant specializes in fresh fish and shellfish grilled on an open charcoal fire. There are excellent-value lunch and early dinner menus.

See map on pp78–9

🔟 North Cornwall

With the Atlantic hammering on its coast, North Cornwall feels harsher than the county's more sheltered southern seaboard. Abandoned engine houses and chimney stacks recall its industrial past, while numerous Wesleyan chapels reveal the faith of its mining population. Between the cliffs are some of the region's best surf beaches. You can enjoy fine seafood in Padstow, explore historic buildings at Prideaux Place and Lanhydrock, and hunt out Arthurian connections, not least the ruins at Tintagel.

Ruins of Tintagel Castle

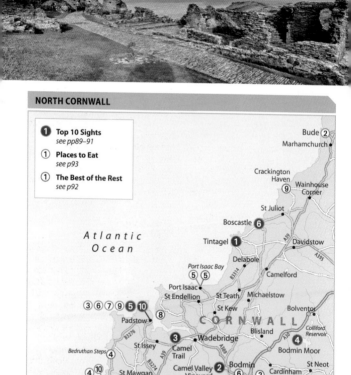

NORTH CORNWALL

① **Top 10 Sights**
see pp89–91

① **Places to Eat**
see p93

① **The Best of the Rest**
see p92

Atlantic Ocean

Bude ②
Marhamchurch •

Crackington Haven
Wainhouse Corner ⑨

St Juliot

Boscastle ⑥

Tintagel ①
Davidstow

Delabole

Camelford

Port Isaac Bay ⑤ ⑤

Port Isaac •
St Endellion
St Teath
Michaelstow

St Kew
Bolventor

③⑥⑦⑨⑤⑩ ⑧
Blisland
Colliford Reservoir

Padstow •

C O R N W A L L

③ • Wadebridge
Bodmin Moor ④

St Issey
Camel Trail

Bedruthan Steps ④
Camel Valley Vineyard ②
Bodmin ⑥
Cardinham
St Neot

④ ⑩
St Mawgan
St Wenn

River Fowey

Watergate Bay
Lanivet ⑨

①⑧⑦⑦⑧
St Columb Major
Lanhydrock

Newquay •
Roche
Lostwithiel

Cubert •
①
Indian Queens

12 miles ⑩ ③ 5 miles
Carthew

0 kilometres   8

0 miles   8

Previous pages Dramatic cliffs at Land's End

1 Tintagel Castle

MAP D2 ▪ Tintagel ▪ 01840 770328 ▪ Open Apr–Sep: 10am–6pm; Oct: 10am–5pm; Nov–Jan: 10am–4pm Sat & Sun; Feb–Mar: Wed–Sun ▪ Adm ▪ www.english-heritage.org.uk

This coastal stronghold is one of the country's most romantic castle ruins. Its appeal is enhanced by its Arthurian associations; it is the supposed birthplace of the Once and Future King. However, the structure probably dates from the 12th century, when it belonged to the Norman earls of Cornwall. There may already have been a Roman fortification and traces of a Celtic monastery have been found here too.

2 Camel Valley Vineyard

MAP D4 ▪ Nanstallon, Bodmin ▪ 01208 77959 ▪ Open Mon–Fri; Easter–Sep: Mon–Sat ▪ www.camel valley.com

Set on the gentle slopes of the Camel Valley, this vineyard, founded in 1989 by an ex-RAF pilot and his wife, is the largest in Cornwall. It produces international prize-winning sparkling wines, and red, white and rosé wines, many of them to be found in the region's top restaurants. Combining traditional methods with innovative New World techniques, it grows a number of grape varieties. Book ahead for the regular weekday tours with wine tasting in season (young adults need to provide proof they are aged 18 or over).

Cyclists on the Camel Trail

3 Camel Trail

MAP E3–D3

This walking and cycling route runs for 27 km (17 miles) between Padstow and the edge of Bodmin Moor. The Padstow–Wadebridge section is on a resurfaced railway track and offers glimpses of the abundant birdlife along the Camel Estuary. From Wadebridge, the route heads southeast towards Bodmin before following the winding river through tranquil woods north to Poley's Bridge. The tourist offices at Padstow, Wadebridge and Bodmin all have leaflets, detailed guides and maps of the route.

4 Bodmin Moor

MAP E3

Cornwall's great inland wilderness is made of the same granite mass as Dartmoor and has the same mixture of rugged grandeur interspersed with splashing rivers and shady woodland. Dotted with mysterious prehistoric remains such as the Hurlers and Trethevy Quoit, the moor has a plethora of places associated with King Arthur and his knights. In the midst of the desolate expanses lie appealing villages, such as Blisland, St Neot's and Altarnun.

Prehistoric remains on Bodmin Moor

Colourful fishing trawlers moored at Padstow's harbour

5 Padstow

Both fishing port and seaside resort, Padstow is also Cornwall's gastronomic capital, synonymous with gourmet food since seafood champion Rick Stein established a restaurant here in the 1970s. The beaches nearby attract both surfers and families, and the sheltered Camel Estuary has great walking and cycling routes *(see pp34–5)*.

6 Boscastle

MAP D2

The great wall of cliffs comprising much of North Cornwall's coast is sliced through here by the Valency and Jordan rivers, which twist through a ravine to a tiny harbour. Boscastle was devastated by a flash flood in 2004, but the damage has been repaired and the village has regained its serenity. Look out for the famous blowhole known as Devil's Bellows, below Penally Point.

Meerkat, Newquay Zoo

7 Newquay's Beaches

MAP C4

Newquay developed as a beach resort after the railway arrived in the 1870s, and is now one of Britain's pre-eminent surf resorts, hosting numerous competitions at Fistral Beach. Holywell Bay and Perran Beach are also highly regarded surfing spots, while the more sheltered Towan Beach, Tolcarne and Lusty Glaze are better for families. Watergate Bay attracts the extreme sports crowd.

8 Newquay Zoo

MAP C4 ▪ Trenance Gardens ▪ 01637 873342 ▪ Times vary ▪ Adm ▪ www. newquayzoo.org.uk

This zoo holds more than 130 species and boasts an active conservation and education agenda. Visitors can meet the animals and watch them being fed. Look out for the graceful red pandas and comical lemurs, and have fun feeding fish to the penguins and mealy worms to the meerkats. There's also a Dragon Maze.

9 Lanhydrock

The finest house in Cornwall was originally Jacobean, but little of it survived a fire in 1881, which makes the Victorian interior visible today – restored by the National Trust – all the more astonishing. It comprises some 50 rooms, including

---

CORNWALL'S MINEWORKS

An iconic image of the Cornish landscape is the engine house and chimney that denote the existence of a former mine. North Cornwall is dotted with these castle-like granite structures, which hark back to a time when the county was producing up to two-thirds of the world's copper and tin. The industry fell into decline in the 1870s.

the cramped maids' quarters and the lavish rooms of the Agar-Robartes family, but the highlights are the impressive kitchens and sculleries. The gardens and wooded parkland are wonderful and worth exploring (see pp12–13).

⑩ Prideaux Place

This mansion blends Elizabethan splendour with 18th-century Gothic. Highlights include the Great Chamber, with biblical tales illustrated on the plaster ceiling, and the oak-panelled Great Hall, with its frieze of animals. Look out for the carving of Elizabeth I standing on a pig (a symbol of vice) next to the fireplace. The morning room has paintings by Cornish artist John Opie (see p34).

Library at Prideaux Place

A DRIVE ALONG CORNWALL'S NORTHERN COAST

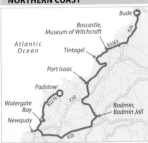

▶ MORNING

Cornwall's northernmost resort of Bude has fine beaches for a morning dip. From here, the A39 plunges south; branch off onto the B3263 to **Boscastle** for a stroll along its harbour and to explore the **Museum of Witchcraft** (see p40). On the way in or out of the village, stop at St Juliot's church, where Thomas Hardy once worked as an architect. Travel 6 km (4 miles) to **Tintagel** (see p89), one of the most popular sights in Cornwall – its ruined castle is said to have been King Arthur's birthplace. After touring the ruins, lunch in a local café, or escape the crowds by heading south to the harbour village of **Port Isaac** (see p92).

AFTERNOON

After lunch, head inland to drive to Bodmin, an ancient market town featuring Cornwall's largest parish church. You can also visit the **Bodmin Jail** (see p92) and the Courtroom Experience next to the tourist office, where you can cast your vote in a re-enactment of a celebrated murder trial of 1844. From Bodmin, take the A30 west to **Newquay**, which has some of Cornwall's best beaches. The county's only zoo is located here too. Head up the coast on the B3276 and stop at **Watergate Bay** (see p52), where the The Beach Hut (see p93) is a great spot for snacks. Surfing equipment can be rented at the Extreme Academy. For dinner, continue up the B3276 to **Padstow**, which boasts a wide range of top-rated seafood restaurants (see p93).

See map on p88 ←

The Best of the Rest

1 Trerice
MAP C4 ▪ Kestle Mill, Newquay
▪ 01637 875404 ▪ Open Mar–Oct:
11am–5pm daily ▪ Adm

This Elizabethan National Trust
manor has a splendid barrel-roofed
Great Chamber. You can play kayles
(Cornish skittles) in the grounds.

2 Cardinham Woods
MAP E3 ▪ Bikes for hire

There are four forest walks and a
waymarked trail for mountain-
bikers in these woods.

3 Callestick Farm
MAP C5
▪ Callestick, Truro
▪ 01872 573126
▪ Open Easter–Oct 10am–
5:30pm Mon–Sat (to 5pm Sun)

Ice cream has been made here since
1953, using clotted cream from the
milk of the farm's cattle. Watch it being
made – and sample it in the café.

4 Bedruthan Steps
MAP C3

The jagged slate outcrops on this
beach were said to be the stepping
stones of the giant Bedruthan.
A cliffside staircase descends to
the beach but bathing is unsafe.

5 Port Isaac
MAP D3

A typical North Cornish fishing
village with winding lanes and a
working harbour. The surrounding
cliffs offer some fine walking.

6 Bodmin Jail
MAP D4 ▪ Berrycombe Rd,
Bodmin ▪ 01208 76292 ▪ Open
9:30am–6pm daily ▪ Adm
▪ www.bodminjail.org

Built in 1779, this former jail is a
fascinating attraction, with tours of the
cells, visits to the "execution pit" and
an After Dark experience at weekends.

7 Blue Reef Aquarium
MAP C4 ▪ Towan Promenade,
Newquay ▪ 01637 878134
▪ Open 10am–4pm daily
(to 5pm summer) ▪ Adm

From sea horses to
octopuses, get up
close to sea crea-
tures in over 40 habitats,
including an ocean tank.

**Turtle at the Blue
Reef Aquarium**

8 St Enodoc
MAP D3 ▪ Daymer Bay ▪ www.
northcornwallclusterofchurches.org.uk

This tiny 13th-century church
appears hidden amid dunes in the
middle of a golf course. The poet
John Betjeman is buried here.

9 Crackington Haven
MAP E2

This scenic beach is backed by
dramatic cliffs rising to 130 m (430 ft),
with strangely contorted rock strata.

10 East Pool Mine
MAP C5 ▪ Pool, Redruth
▪ 01209 315027 ▪ Open mid-Mar–
Oct 10:30am–5pm Tue–Sat ▪ Adm

Two beam engines are preserved in
their engine houses at this museum.

Clifftops above Port Isaac

Places to Eat

PRICE CATEGORIES

For a three-course meal for one with half a bottle of wine, including taxes and extra charges.

£ under £35 ■ ££ £35–£55 ■ £££ over £55

1 Lewinnick Lodge
MAP C4 ■ Pentire Headland, Newquay ■ 01637 878117 ■ Open from 10am daily ■ ££

Seafood is the speciality at this coastal restaurant. Take in the views from the terrace or dine in the main restaurant, bar or beer garden.

2 Life's a Beach
MAP E2 ■ Summerleaze Beach, Bude ■ 01288 355222 ■ ££

Overlooking the Atlantic, this café serves baguettes and burgers during the day. By night it is a classy candlelit bistro with a focus on seafood.

3 Paul Ainsworth at No. 6
MAP D3 ■ 6 Middle St, Padstow ■ 01841 532093 ■ Closed Sun & Mon ■ £££

Dress up for dining in this Georgian town house with contemporary decor and sophisticated food.

4 Fifteen
MAP C4 ■ Watergate Bay ■ 01637 861000 ■ £££

A bevy of young chefs show their culinary expertise in this Jamie Oliver restaurant that overlooks the beach.

5 Restaurant Nathan Outlaw
MAP D3 ■ 6 New Rd, Port Isaac ■ 01208 880896 ■ Closed Sun–Tue ■ £££

Chef and writer Nathan Outlaw's flagship fish and seafood restaurant serves a single set tasting menu based around the morning's catch.

6 Stein's Fish & Chips
MAP D3 ■ South Quay, Padstow ■ 01841 532700 ■ £

The most affordable and relaxed of Stein's eateries, this place has some of the most succulent fish and chips in the West Country. Check out Stein's Fisheries and Seafood Bar next door.

7 The Seafood Restaurant
MAP D3 ■ Riverside, Padstow ■ 01841 532700 ■ £££

A joyous gastronomic experience in a lively restaurant whose walls are covered with paintings. The menu features dishes familiar from Rick Stein's books and TV programmes, along with newer creations.

The Seafood Restaurant

8 Rick Stein Fistral
MAP C4 ■ Fistral Beach, Newquay ■ 01637 303103 ■ £

Casual eating – the food is served in cardboard boxes – in a stunning setting above crashing waves. Enjoy a range of dishes, from classic fish and chips to pad thai and Goan chicken curry.

9 St Petroc's Bistro
MAP D3 ■ 4 New St, Padstow ■ 01841 532700 ■ ££

Smaller than the Seafood Restaurant, this Stein venture has fewer choices on the menu and lower prices, but delivers the goods. Meat is given equal billing with seafood.

10 The Beach Hut
MAP C4 ■ Watergate Bay ■ 01637 860877 ■ ££

With its stunning beachside location, this is a casual place for summer evenings. Fish specials and burgers are mainstays of the menu.

See map on p88

TOP 10 South Cornwall

With its indented coastline and river estuaries interspersed with small settlements, South Cornwall is ripe for exploration. Fowey and fishing villages such as Polperro should not be missed, while Cornwall's capital, Truro, is small enough to negotiate on foot. The region's most famous attraction is the Eden Project, although South Cornwall's other major gardens, Trelissick and Heligan, are also essential stops. To the south, the Roseland Peninsula offers sandy coves and plenty of places to stay, eat and drink.

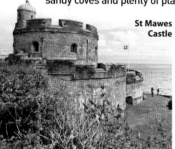

St Mawes Castle

1 St Mawes Castle

MAP C5 ▪ St Mawes ▪ 01326 270526 ▪ Open Apr–Sep: 10am–6pm daily; Oct: 10am–5pm daily; Nov–Feb: 10am–4pm Sat & Sun; Mar: 10am–4pm Wed–Sun ▪ Adm ▪ www.english-heritage.org.uk

The lesser of the two 16th-century artillery forts close to the Fal Estuary, this castle is better preserved than Pendennis, with heraldic devices dedicated to Henry VIII and Edward VI.

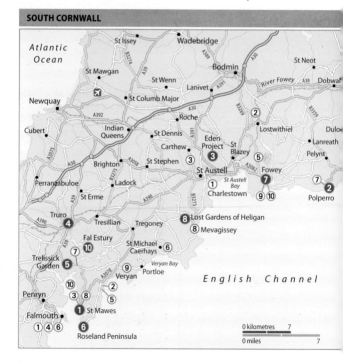

SOUTH CORNWALL

Atlantic Ocean

St Issey · Wadebridge
St Mawgan
St Wenn · Bodmin · St Neot
Newquay
St Columb Major · Lanivet · River Fowey · Dobwa
Cubert · Roche
Indian Queens · St Dennis · Lostwithiel · Dulo
Carthew · Eden Project · Lanreath
Brighton · St Stephen · St Blazey · Pelynt
Perranzabuloe · Ladock · St Austell · Fowey
St Erme · Charlestown · St Austell Bay · Polperro
Truro · Tresillian · Tregoney · Lost Gardens of Heligan
Fal Estury · Mevagissey
Trelissick Garden · St Michael Caerhays
Penryn · Veryan · Veryan Bay · Portloe
Falmouth · St Mawes
Roseland Peninsula

English Channel

0 kilometres 7
0 miles 7

The pretty village of Polperro, set around a fishing harbour

The interior has 19th-century ships' cannons plus a cannon from c.1560, recovered off the Devon coast.

2 Polperro
MAP E4

At peak times, this Cornish fishing village is overcrowded, but visit out of season, or early in the morning, and you can appreciate its charm. A long main street leads down to a huddle of houses around the harbour. Check out the smuggling and fishing museum housed in an old pilchard factory.

3 Eden Project

Since opening in a former clay pit in 2001, this has been one of Cornwall's success stories. A "living theatre of plants and people", it is a great illustration of the diversity of the planet's plant life and makes for a perfect visit at any time of year (see pp14–15).

4 Royal Cornwall Museum
MAP C5 ■ River St, Truro ■ 01872 272205 ■ Open 10am–4:45pm Tue–Sat, 10am–4pm Sun, public hols

This museum is a cornucopia of Cornish culture, with everything from Bronze Age pottery to Newlyn art and minerals and fossils collections. Botanical and zoological specimens include stuffed puffins, butterflies and shells.

Exhibits at the Royal Cornwall Museum

View of the Fal at Trelissick Garden

5 Trelissick Garden

This lovely, extensive garden has lawns, flowerbeds and hollows filled with rare plants and shrubs, sprawling parkland and miles of woodland paths with panoramic views of the River Fal. Late April, early May and September are the best times to visit (see p19). The King Harry chain ferry, supposedly founded by King Henry VIII after spending his honeymoon with Anne Boleyn in St Mawes, crosses the River Fal below the garden, allowing direct access to the Roseland Peninsula – the round trip by road is 43 km (27 miles) (see p19).

6 Roseland Peninsula
MAP C5

A long, broad peninsula stretching south of Truro to bank the Fal Estuary, the Roseland Peninsula has lush rolling hills, subtropical gardens and unspoiled sandy coves, making it one of Cornwall's most desirable destinations. There are

chic hotels and restaurants along the coast and in St Mawes, while the church of St-Just-in-Roseland is set in a lavish subtropical garden, described by the poet Sir John Betjeman as "the most beautiful churchyard on earth". Portscatho, the sandy cove of Porthcurnick, the long sands at Towan and St Anthony's Head Lighthouse are among the peninsula's coastal highlights.

7 Fowey
MAP E4

Climbing up the west bank of the River Fowey, this was one of the foremost ports of medieval England and is still a busy harbour town. Most of today's maritime activity, however, involves the pleasure boats anchored in the estuary. It is worth hiring a boat to fully enjoy the beauty of the river.

8 Lost Gardens of Heligan
MAP D4 ■ Pentewan, St Austell ■ 01726 845100 ■ Open Apr–Sep: 10am–6pm daily; Oct–Mar: 10am–5pm daily ■ Adm ■ www.heligan.com

"Lost" for 70 years and neglected for even longer, this salvaged Victorian garden is a triumph of horticultural design. Presenting a splendid pag-eantry of plants in a variety of habitats, including ferneries, fruit houses, Italian gardens and a kitchen garden, this subtropical "Jungle" and "Lost Valley", with its strong emphasis on conservation, appeals to both adults and kids.

Hikers on the Roseland Peninsula

9 Cotehele House
MAP H5 ▪ St Dominick, Saltash
▪ 01579 351346 ▪ Open mid-Mar–
Oct: 11am–5pm daily ▪ Adm

The excellent condition of this Tudor abode is due to its abandonment by its owners, the Edgcumbe family, who left it intact for a more accessible home outside Plymouth. It remained in the family until the National Trust took it over in 1947. The house has many original pieces of furniture, suits of armour, and a collection of embroideries and tapestries that are best seen on a bright day as the rooms have no electric light.

Façade at Cotehele House

10 Fal (Carrick Roads) Estuary
The largest of Cornwall's tidal river estuaries, the Fal is an ancient river valley, drowned at the end of the last ice age, when glaciers melted. From its source near St Austell, the Fal meets up with five other rivers and numerous small tidal creeks to flow into the estuary. It is 34 m (140 ft) at its deepest point. Along the river are more than 4,500 moorings for crafts, from yachts to deep water freighters, which often congregate here between contracts (see pp18–19).

THE CHINA CLAY STORY
No one passing through the St Austell area can fail to notice the vast conical spoil heaps linked to the local china clay industry. The substance is used in a variety of products, from paint and paper to medicines. You can learn about its history and applications at the fascinating Wheal Martyn (see p98).

A DRIVING TOUR IN SOUTH CORNWALL

▶ MORNING

Start your journey in Looe, a traditional resort that has gained a reputation as a shark-fishing centre. A 6-km (4-mile) drive from here takes you to **Polperro** (see p95), whose tightly packed houses and minuscule harbour are best appreciated before the crowds arrive. There is a small smuggling and fishing museum here. From Polperro, a scenic minor road leads you west to Bodinnick village, where regular ferries cross to **Fowey**. The port town has a selection of pubs and bistros that make for a good lunch stop (there is a car park near the ferry quay). Before or after eating, take a stroll around Fowey to see St Catherine's Castle, one of Henry VIII's fortifications, or follow the 6-km (4-mile) Hall Walk, climbing through woodland above the harbour to Penleath Point for tremendous views.

AFTERNOON

From Fowey, take the A3082 to St Austell, from which the A390, B3287 and A3078 will bring you to St Mawes on the **Fal (Carrick Roads) Estuary**. Here, **St Mawes Castle** (see p94) offers river views. If you have time, explore the **Roseland Peninsula** (see p96), an area of backwaters and churches. North of St Mawes, **Trelissick Garden** offers captivating woodland walks. The King Harry ferry crosses the river, from where it is a short drive to the county capital, Truro. Dominated by its Neo-Gothic cathedral, it has good restaurants and accommodation, and an excellent museum.

See map on pp94–5 ←

The Best of the Rest

Elegant exterior of 19th-century Caerhays Castle, near St Austell

① Shipwreck and Heritage Centre
MAP D4 ■ Quay Rd, Charlestown ■ 01726 69897 ■ Open Mar–Oct: 10am–5pm daily ■ Adm ■ www.shipwreckcharlestown.com
This collection holds discoveries from some 150 shipwrecks, including memorabilia from the *Titanic*.

② Restormel Castle
MAP E4 ■ Lostwithiel ■ 01208 872687 ■ Open Apr–Sep: 10am–5pm daily; Jul & Aug: to 6pm; Oct: to 4pm ■ Adm ■ www.english-heritage.org.uk
The parapet of this 13th-century keep has great views over the Fowey Valley.

③ Wheal Martyn
MAP D4 ■ Wheal Martyn, St Austell ■ 01726 850362 ■ Apr–Oct: 10am–5pm daily (Nov–Mar: to 4pm) ■ Adm ■ www.wheal-martyn.com
This museum provides a fascinating insight into the china clay industry.

④ Mount Edgcumbe
MAP F4 ■ Cremyll, Torpoint ■ 01752 822236 ■ Open Apr–Sep: 11am–4:30pm Sun–Thu ■ Adm ■ www.mountedgcumbe.gov.uk
Rebuilt after World War II, this 16th-century house displays Chinese porcelain and Flemish tapestries.

⑤ Castle Dore
MAP E4 ■ Golant
This Iron Age hillfort, with its concentric rings of defensive ridges, is considered to be the site of the palace of the legendary figure, King Mark of Cornwall.

⑥ Caerhays Castle
MAP D5 ■ Gorran, St Austell ■ 01872 501310 ■ Tours mid-Mar–mid-Jun: 11:30am, 1pm, 2:30pm Mon–Fri ■ Adm ■ www.caerhays.co.uk
Take a guided tour of this 19th-century castle, an elegant backdrop to Porthluney Cove beach.

⑦ King Harry Ferry
MAP C5 ■ Feock, Truro ■ 01872 863132 ■ www.falriver.co.uk
Shave miles off the road trip between St Mawes and Falmouth by taking this chain ferry across the Fal.

⑧ Mevagissey
MAP D5
With its long tradition of fishing and smuggling, this busy port is worth visiting for its good museum, pubs and seafood restaurants.

⑨ Veryan
MAP D5
Close to good beaches, Veryan is known for its 200-year-old circular houses designed to prevent the devil from hiding in corners.

⑩ Carrick Roads Estuary
MAP C5
This estuary complex is one of the world's largest natural harbours, with lovely coastal walks and sandy coves.

Places to Eat

1 **The Wheel House**
MAP C5 ■ Upton Slip, Falmouth ■ 01326 318050 ■ Open Wed–Sat for dinner ■ No credit cards ■ ££
This quayside shellfish café serves simple oyster, mussel, prawn and crab dishes in *cataplanas* (Portuguese dishes), plus house wine.

2 **Driftwood Restaurant**
MAP C5 ■ Rosevine, Portscatho ■ 01872 580644 ■ Dinner only ■ £££
Fresh seafood and local meat dishes are the mainstays of the menu at this elegant hotel-restaurant perched above the sea, offering fine views.

3 **St Mawes Hotel**
MAP C5 ■ Commercial Rd, St Mawes ■ 01326 270 266 ■ ££
A relaxed brasserie serving simple dishes at lunch and dinner, such as lobster and chips and home-made pizza using local ingredients. Popular for an evening prosecco or cocktail.

Bar area at St Mawes Hotel

4 **Hooked on the Rocks**
MAP C5 ■ Swanpool Beach, Falmouth ■ 01326 311886 ■ ££
The panoramic beachside terrace here is a great place to enjoy a selection of tapas, lobster or crab, or Cornish bouillabaisse.

5 **The Hidden Hut**
MAP C5 ■ Porthcurnick Beach, Portscatho, Truro ■ £
A much-loved beach café in a hut perched above sandy Porthcurnick cove, serving simple lunches, soups, coffees and cakes, with occasional Friday feast nights *(see p61)*.

6 **Gylly Café**
MAP C5 ■ Cliff Rd, Falmouth ■ 01326 312884 ■ ££
A heavenly place for breakfast, lunch, cakes or dinner, with splendid views over Gyllyngvase Beach. This is a Falmouth institution.

7 **The Kitchen**
MAP E4 ■ The Coombes, Polperro ■ 01503 272812 ■ Closed Mon & Jan ■ ££
This simple, intimate restaurant serves excellent fish and meat dishes, plus delicious clotted cream desserts and Cornish cheeses.

8 **Hotel Tresanton**
MAP C5 ■ 27 Lower Castle Rd, St Mawes ■ 01326 270055 ■ £££
Modern Mediterranean food is served in this seaside hotel *(see p118)*. A terrace offers scenic alfresco dining.

9 **Q Restaurant**
MAP E4 ■ Old Quay House, 28 Fore St, Fowey ■ 01726 833302 ■ Closed Mon & Tue lunch, Easter–Sep; times vary in winter ■ £££
This restaurant at the Old Quay House hotel *(see p116)*, enjoys splendid views over the River Fowey and fabulous food to match.

10 **Dwelling House**
MAP E4 ■ 6 Fore St, Fowey ■ 01726 833662 ■ £
The tiers of scrumptious cakes and delectable scones on view in the window of this period tearoom lure visitors inside. There's a menu of leaf teas to complement your chosen treat.

See map on pp94–5

PRICE CATEGORIES
For a three-course meal for one with half a bottle of wine, including taxes and extra charges.
....
£ under £35   ££ £35–£55   £££ over £55

⒑ West Cornwall and the Isles of Scilly

Egyptian House detail, Penzance

For many, the western tip of Cornwall embodies what makes the county so special. Here you can find every kind of landscape and settlement Cornwall has to offer, from the port of Falmouth to the fishing hamlet of Mousehole, from the bare moorland of the Penwith Peninsula to sandy Whitesand Bay and the inhospitable cliffs at Zennor. There are prehistoric remains and the island stronghold of St Michael's Mount. Land's End and Lizard Point bring you face-to-face with the raging Atlantic Ocean, but you can get closer still by venturing out to the beautiful Isles of Scilly.

WEST CORNWALL AND THE ISLES OF SCILLY

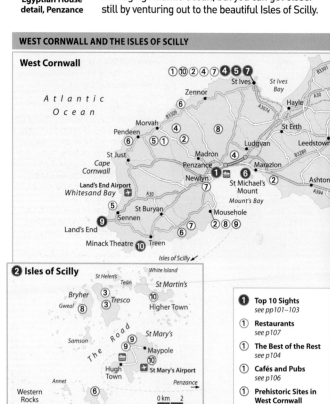

①	**Top 10 Sights** see pp101–103
①	**Restaurants** see p107
①	**The Best of the Rest** see p104
①	**Cafés and Pubs** see p106
①	**Prehistoric Sites in West Cornwall** see p105

1 Penzance

Draped over a hill above a harbour, charming Penzance possesses two of Cornwall's best museum-galleries – Penlee House and the Exchange – and plenty of historical character in the handsome buildings of Chapel Street. From the town, all the glories of the Penwith Peninsula are easily accessible, from St Michael's Mount to the coast's rocky coves and beaches (see pp32–3).

2 Isles of Scilly

It takes effort to reach the Isles of Scilly but few come away disappointed. Imagined by some to be the remains of the legendary lost land of Lyonnesse, which sank below the waves after the last battle

Boats off Bryer Island, Isles of Scilly

between Arthur and Mordred, this scattered archipelago is breathtakingly beautiful, sprinkled with hundreds of tiny, jagged rocks and islets. Of the five inhabited islands, the main island is St Mary's. The chicest retreat is privately owned Tresco, home to the Abbey Gardens, while Bryher, St Martin's and St Agnes appeal to those who want to escape from contemporary life.

3 Trebah Gardens

Subtropical Trebah is one of the most beautiful gardens in Cornwall, spilling down to the verdant waters of the River Helford. Now owned by the National Trust, the gardens were created by Charles Fox, a Quaker, scientist and owner of an iron foundry, who paid meticulous attention to every detail. Highlights include valleys of hydrangeas and azaleas, a water garden and a river beach (see p18).

Footpath through Trebah Gardens

4 Tate St Ives

A beacon of modern art, this gallery pays homage to the local schools of art that have flourished in the area, while also showcasing contemporary work. Converted from a gasworks in 1993, the building is a modernist statement in itself, with a rooftop terrace offering stunning ocean views. An extension, doubling gallery space, was unveiled in 2017 (see p30).

5 Barbara Hepworth Museum and Sculpture Garden

One of the foremost sculptors of the 20th century, Hepworth was inspired by the granite landscapes of West Cornwall and settled in St Ives in 1939. Her sleek, abstract sculptures can be seen in her former St Ives studio. Smaller works are displayed inside, while the adjoining walled garden provides an ideal setting for her large-scale geometric forms (see p30).

STARGAZY PIE

According to legend, after a winter of storms when boats had been unable to put out to sea, Mousehole's people were starving. On 23 December, fisherman Tom Bawcock braved the storm and landed a huge catch of pilchards, which were then cooked up by the villagers into stargazy pie.

---

6 St Michael's Mount

This castle residence in Mount's Bay can be reached by causeway or passenger ferry, followed by a steep climb up to the house itself. Inside, the most impressive rooms are the Tudor Great Hall and the dainty Blue Drawing Room. Other rooms hold armour, weaponry and memorabilia. Views from the battlements are stupendous (see pp32–3).

St Michael's Mount

Boats at St Ives' sandy waterfront

7 St Ives

This seaside town has a distinctly Mediterranean flavour, with its maze of flowery lanes climbing up the hill. The clear light and rugged landscape were a major draw for a succession of artists who settled here, renting studios from local fishermen. Today, tourists have replaced pilchards as the town's mainstay, thronging its numerous galleries, sandy beaches and elegant restaurants every summer. To escape the crowds, climb up to the Island, a grassy headland with views across St Ives Bay (see pp30–31).

8 Lizard Peninsula
MAP C6–B6

As the southernmost peninsula in Britain, the Lizard is an area of extreme contrasts, stretching from the glassy waters, whitewashed villages and ancient oak wood-land of the River Helford, across open heathland to serpentine cliffs, dramatic sculpted bays and unspoiled fishing villages such as Cadgwith Cove. On the southwest edge of bleak Goonhilly Downs is stunning Kynance Cove.

9 Land's End
MAP A6

The westernmost tip of the British mainland holds a perennial fascination. The headland offers panoramic views over the coast and to rocky outcrops out at sea with, intriguing names such as Dr Syntax Head and the Armed Knight. The Longships lighthouse, 2 km (1 mile) out, is also usually visible. At times you can spot Wolf Rock lighthouse, 15 km (9 miles) to the southwest, and even the Isles of Scilly, 45 km (28 miles) away.

View from Minack Theatre

10 Minack Theatre

The vision of one woman, Rowena Cade (see p28), the Minack is a unique attraction in Cornwall. Just like a Roman amphitheatre on some Mediterranean shore, the theatre has been carved out of the cliff-face above the sea, creating a magical setting for watching plays and musicals. Shows are performed from April through to September, though the Exhibition Centre is open all year. Cancellations due to bad weather are rare, but it's advisable to wrap up warmly (see pp28–9).

A WALK FROM NEWLYN TO PORTHCURNO

▶ MORNING

If you're in **Newlyn** (see p104) early enough, look in on the fish auction that takes place here every morning. Start your walk along a cycle-path running south from the harbour. After walking about 2 km (1 mile), you will reach the bijou fishing village of **Mousehole** (pronounced "mowzel") (see p104). The place was ransacked by a Spanish raiding party in 1595, who reputedly left just one building standing – the 14th-century Keigwin House, which is still there. Walk through the village and pick up the coast path heading south to reach Point Spaniard where the raiders supposedly landed. The path then swerves inland before meeting the coast again at Carn Du, the eastern point of Lamorna Cove. Stop for a hearty lunch at the Lamorna Wink pub.

AFTERNOON

From Lamorna the path sticks close to the rocky coast. Follow it past Tater Du lighthouse and round Boscawen Point to St Loy's Cove. For this stretch of the walk there are no cafés, so make sure you stock up with snacks. After a short walk, mainly on the clifftop, you will reach unspoiled Penberth Cove – little more than a few cottages and fishing boats. Continue along the clifftop, past the Iron Age fort of **Treryn Dinas** (see p28), where you can see the famous **Logan Rock** (see p29). For dinner, follow the path down to **Porthcurno** (see pp28–9), which has a café and pub, plus a museum of telegraphy and the **Minack Theatre**.

See map on pp100–101 ←

The Best of the Rest

1 **National Seal Sanctuary**
MAP B5 ■ Gweek, Helston
■ 01326 221361 ■ Open Apr–Oct:
10am–5pm daily; Nov–Apr:
11am–4pm daily ■ Adm
Sick or injured seals are brought
here from all over the country. You
can tour the pools and the hospital.

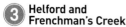
Mousehole's sheltered harbour

2 **Mousehole**
MAP A5
With its steep, cobbled alleyways
and higgledy-piggledy whitewashed
houses, popular Mousehole is the
quintessential Cornish fishing village.

3 **Helford and
Frenchman's Creek**
MAP C5
The whitewashed village of Helford
is the starting point for an easy circular
walk through dense oak woodland to
Frenchman's Creek, named after the
novel by Daphne du Maurier.

4 **Tremenheere Sculpture
Gardens**
MAP B5 ■ Gulval, Penzance ■ 01736
448089 ■ Open mid-Feb–Oct: 10am–
4pm daily ■ Adm
Contemporary sculpture and art
installations blend with lush subtropical planting in a sheltered valley.

5 **Helford Passage**
MAP C5
This pretty village lies across the
river from Helford. The Ferryboat Inn
terrace is a great place to watch the
local gig rowers training.

6 **Geevor Tin Mine**
MAP A5 ■ Trewellard, Pendeen,
St Just ■ 01736 788662 ■ Open Apr–
Oct: 9am–5pm Sun–Fri; Nov–Mar:
10am–4pm Sun–Fri ■ Adm
Tour the surface works and the
18th-century tunnels at the UK's
largest preserved tin mining site.

7 **Newlyn**
MAP A5
As Britain's most important fishing
port, this small town was home to
an influential art movement in the
late 19th and early 20th centuries.
Artists Henry Scott Tuke and Stanhope Forbes provide the core of the
Newlyn Art Gallery's collection.

8 **Glendurgan**
MAP C5 ■ Mawnan Smith
■ 01326 252020 ■ Open mid-Feb–
Oct: 10:30am–5:30pm or dusk Tue–
Sun (daily in Aug) ■ Adm
Highlights of this lovely 19th-century
wooded garden include azalea and
camellia gardens and a popular
cherry laurel hedge maze (see p51).

9 **Western Rocks,
Isles of Scilly**
MAP A4
These remote islands are breeding
grounds for grey seals and several
seabird species. Landing is prohib-
ited, but there are boat trips to see
shipwrecks and spot birds and seals.

10 **Lizard Lighthouse**
MAP C6 ■ 3 Lighthouse Rd,
Lizard, Helston ■ 01326 290202 ■ Open
Apr–Oct: 11am–5pm Sun–Thu ■ Adm
Climb the southernmost lighthouse
in mainland Britain for displays on
morse code, semaphore and sounding
foghorns. It's also a bird-watching site.

See map on pp100–101

Prehistoric Sites in West Cornwall

1 Chun Castle
MAP A5 ■ Near Morvah, off B3318

The walls of this Iron Age hillfort are mainly collapsed, but in parts they reach a height of 3 m (9 ft), and the gateposts still stand. The ruined huts inside date from the Dark Ages.

2 Lanyon Quoit
MAP A5 ■ Near Morvah

Also known as the Giant's Quoit or Giant's Table, this capped burial chamber is one of the most accessible of West Penwith's prehistoric remains.

3 Halliggye Fogou
MAP C6 ■ Trelowarren, Mawgan, Helston ■ Open daily

This is one of the most impressive of West Cornwall's *fogous* – long underground structures from the Iron Age.

4 Men-an-Tol
MAP A5 ■ Near Morvah, off Morvah–Madron Road

The Cornish name (which means stone-with-a-hole) very accurately describes this Bronze Age monument that was long thought to have mystical healing powers. Situated on moorland, it is 2,500–4,000 years old.

5 Chun Quoit
MAP A5 ■ Near Morvah, off B3318

On open moorland, this quoit – a neolithic chamber tomb topped by a flat stone and resembling a giant granite mushroom – dates from around 2,000 BC.

6 Tregiffian Burial Chamber
MAP A6 ■ Near Lamorna, off B3315

This barrow tomb revealed a funerary urn and cremated bones when it was excavated in 1967.

7 The Merry Maidens
MAP A6 ■ Near Lamorna, off B3315

Considered Cornwall's most perfect stone circle. According to legend, it is the remains of 19 maidens turned to stone for carousing on the Sabbath.

8 Chysauster
MAP A5 ■ Near Zennor ■ 07831 757934 ■ Open Apr–Oct ■ Adm

Cornwall's most complete prehistoric monument consists of stone-walled houses arranged around courtyards, where you can discern a number of hearths, basins and drains.

9 Bant's Carn, Isles of Scilly
MAP B4 ■ Halangy Down, St Mary's

One of the Isles' many megalithic monuments, this atmospheric burial chamber on St Mary's has a roof comprising four huge slabs.

10 Porth Hellick Barrow, Isles of Scilly
MAP B4 ■ Porth Hellick Down, St Mary's

Located in the southeastern corner of St Mary's island, this is the best-preserved of the prehistoric tombs on the Isles of Scilly.

Chun Quoit

Cafés and Pubs

1 Pedn Olva

This contemporary pub belongs to the St Austell Brewery and is set high on the promontory between St Ives' two beaches. Try the local goat's cheese with a local beer – it's unforgettable. Accommodation is also available *(see pp116–19)*.

2 Victoria Inn

MAP B5 ▪ Perranuthnoe
▪ 01736 710309

This pink-painted pub has a cosy bar and a popular restaurant next door, serving locally inspired dishes.

3 New Inn

MAP A4 ▪ Tresco, Isles of Scilly
▪ 01720 423006

A stylish pub with dining in a courtyard as well as inside. Offers superior pub food, such as Bryher lobster and chips or Tresco partridge sausage roll.

4 Blue Anchor Inn

MAP B5 ▪ 50 Coinagehall St, Helston ▪ 01326 562821

Enjoy the medieval atmosphere at this former monks' resthouse dating from the 15th century. Cosy nooks and home-brewed Spingo ales are the main attractions.

5 Kynance Cove

MAP B5 ▪ Kynance Cove, Helston ▪ 01326 290436

A beach café in a former fisherman's cottage – the decked terrace is the perfect place to relax and watch the dramatic cove change with the rise and fall of the tide.

6 Turk's Head

MAP A4 ▪ St Agnes, Isles of Scilly ▪ 01720 422434

The most southwesterly pub in Britain has views of the sea and a community hub, serving Turks Ale, crab rolls and great Cornish pasties.

7 Ferry Boat Inn

MAP C5 ▪ Helford Passage
▪ 01326 250625

With a terrace overlooking the River Helford, the hearty lunches and lighter snacks here are popular with walkers on the coastal path.

8 Crab Shack

MAP A4 ▪ Bryher, Isles of Scilly
▪ 01722 422947 ▪ Closed Oct–Apr

Pop on a pinny, roll up your sleeves and dig into mussels, scallops or crabs, with chips, salad and wine at this simple wooden shack.

9 Ship Inn

MAP A5 ▪ South Cliff, Mousehole
▪ 01736 731234

You can almost feel the sea spray in this fisherman's pub above the harbour, full of maritime character. Battered catch of the day with chips is usually on the menu.

10 Porthmeor Beach Café

MAP B5 ▪ Porthmeor, St Ives
▪ 01736 793366

This chic café, located just above Porthmeor Beach, affords great views. The imaginative food is inspired by far-flung cuisines and the dessert tapas are sublime.

Kynance Cove

Restaurants

PRICE CATEGORIES

For a three-course meal for one with half a bottle of wine, including taxes and extra charges.

£ under £35 ■ ££ £35–55 ■ £££ over £55

1 Kota Restaurant
MAP B5 ■ Harbour Rd, Porthleven ■ 01326 562407 ■ Closed Mon & Sun ■ ££

The Chinese-Maori-Malaysian chef Jude adds imaginative twists to dishes made using organic produce at this harbourside restaurant.

2 Blas Burgerworks
MAP B5 ■ The Warren, St Ives ■ 01736 797272 ■ £

St Ives' lively gourmet burger restaurant serves some excellent chargrilled Cornish burgers. Vegetarian options include a black bean burger and grilled halloumi.

3 The Ruin Beach Café
MAP B4 ■ Tresco, Isles of Scilly ■ 01720 424849 ■ £

Beautifully styled restaurant housed in a former smugglers' cottage, with terrace seating and a contemporary Mediterranean menu, including pizzas from a wood-burning oven.

4 Porthminster Beach Café
MAP B5 ■ Porthminster Beach, St Ives ■ 01736 795352 ■ Closed Mon in winter ■ ££

A beach café by day and a smart and pricey restaurant at night, this place serves dishes such as monkfish curry or crispy squid with miso dressing.

5 Ben Tunnicliffe at Sennen Cove
MAP A5 ■ Sennen Cove ■ 01736 871191 ■ ££

An informal beachside brasserie created by the Michelin-starred chef. From the full English brunch to a shellfish sharing platter, this is simple food prepared brilliantly.

6 Gurnard's Head
MAP A5 ■ Zennor ■ 01736 796928 ■ ££

A stylish, relaxed gastro-pub serving Mediterranean dishes using fresh fish and locally sourced meat and produce.

Gurnard's Head, Zennor

7 Alba
MAP B5 ■ Wharf Rd, St Ives ■ 01736 797222 ■ ££

Fine-dining option with à la carte and set menus, plus dishes for children.

8 2 Fore Street
MAP A5 ■ 2 Fore St, Mousehole ■ 01736 731164 ■ Closed Jan–mid-Feb: Mon & Tue ■ ££

Head to this relaxed French-style bistro right by the harbour for unfussy dishes such as Newlyn crab soufflé.

9 Juliet's Garden Restaurant
MAP B4 ■ St Mary's, Isles of Scilly ■ 01720 422228 ■ Closed Nov–Mar ■ ££

A casual, modern place with outdoor tables and lovely sea views. Enjoy a daytime snack or a candle-lit dinner.

10 Adam's Fish and Chips
MAP B4 ■ Higher Town, St Martin's ■ 01720 423082 ■ Closed Oct–Mar ■ £

Booking is essential at this local spot. Choose your own fish in advance.

See map on pp100–101

Streetsmart

**Surfboards at Polzeath Beach,
North Cornwall**

Getting To and Around Cornwall and Devon

Arriving by Air

The region's main airport is **Exeter Airport**, with direct flights from several UK and European cities. **Newquay Airport** and **Land's End Airport** have year-round flights to St Mary's Airport in the Scilly Isles, and there are seasonal flights from Exeter. The main airline serving the region is **FlyBe**, with **Skybus** operating all flights to the Scilly Isles. For the best deals on fares on all routes, make sure you book well in advance.

Regular buses operated by **Stagecoach** connect Exeter Airport with Exeter St David's railway station, Exeter bus station and Exmouth. There is also a regular bus service between Newquay Airport, Newquay railway station and Padstow, operated by **First Kernow**. A bus service from Land's End Airport to Penzance railway station is operated for Skybus passengers. Minibuses meet arrivals at St Mary's Airport, with transfers to several points on the island.

Arriving by Train

Great Western Railway runs trains along the main line from London Paddington to Penzance, taking approximately 5 hours, usually calling at Exeter, Totnes, Bodmin, Plymouth, Liskeard, Truro and St Erth. The best way to travel is on a sleeper train (the Night Riviera Sleeper), but there is also a good daytime service.

There are several useful branch lines. From Exeter, trains travel south to Torquay and Paignton and north to Barnstaple. From Liskeard, a line heads to Looe. There is also a branch line running north to Newquay from Par, and a very regular service from Truro along the branch line to Falmouth.

Tickets are cheaper when bought well in advance. For multiple journeys, you can save money with Day Ranger tickets, which give one day's unlimited rail travel within Devon (£12) or Cornwall (£13), or Freedom of Devon and Cornwall passes, which offer unlimited rail travel within the region for 3 days out of 7, or 8 days out of 15.

Arriving by Road

In summer and on Bank Holiday weekends, large numbers of drivers – many towing caravans (trailers) – travel along the M5 motorway and A38 trunk road through Devon, and on the A30 and A39 through Cornwall, so progress can be slow.

National Express coaches run from London to Penzance, but the trip takes at least 8 hours and 35 minutes. There are also services to destinations such as Exeter, Truro and Falmouth. Tickets are usually cheaper if bought online in advance.

Arriving by Sea

Brittany Ferries links Plymouth with Roscoff in France and Santander in Spain. From April to October, **Isles of Scilly Travel** runs ferries from Penzance to the islands. The *MS Oldenberg*, operated by the **Lundy Shore Office**, sails to Lundy Island from Ilfracombe and Bideford from April to October.

Getting Around by Bus

Bus services, especially in rural areas, are infrequent, but if time is not an issue, buses can be a scenic and cheap way to tour the region. There are numerous companies in Devon (all listed on the **Devon County Council** website), while in Cornwall most services are run by First Kernow, with a few tiny local operators (listed on the **Cornwall County Council** website). Several companies offer passes for unlimited travel over 1, 3 or 7 days.

Getting Around by Train

Branch lines make it possible to see a fair amount of Cornwall and Devon by train. There are some spectacular routes, some of which run steam trains (see pp56–7).

Getting Around on Foot

The **South West Coast Path** borders the entire

southwest peninsula, while Bodmin Moor, Exmoor and Dartmoor are ideal for inland hikes. There are a number of coast-to-coast walks in both Devon and Cornwall (see pp54–5).

Getting Around by Bike

You can cycle the whole peninsula. Off-road routes include the Granite Way on Dartmoor, as well as the Tarka Trail, the flat Camel Trail and the Saints Way (see pp54–5). Excellent cycle maps and guides are published by **Sustrans** and the **National Cycle Network**.

Getting Around by Car

Once within Devon and Cornwall, most major roads are inland, away from the rugged serrated coastline of the north, and the deep river valleys and rolling peninsulas of the south. Allow plenty of time if travelling by car along the region's labyrinth of narrow lanes. Satnavs often don't work, and many minor roads do not appear on road maps, so if you want to explore a small area in detail, use an OS 1:25,000 map. There is a toll charged to cross the Tamar Bridge from Cornwall into Devon.

Getting Around by River Ferry

Local car ferries across rivers and estuaries often save drivers a detour. The **Kingswear Ferry** avoids the route around the River Dart to reach Dartmouth, while the historic **King Harry** chain ferry between the Roseland Peninsula and Trelissick saves drivers 43 km (27 miles). **C Toms & Son** runs a useful car ferry between Fowey and Bodinnick. **Padstow Ferry** shuttles passengers between Padstow and Rock, and in summer **Mevagissey Ferries** runs a passenger ferry between Fowey and Mevagissey.

DIRECTORY

ARRIVING BY AIR

Exeter Airport
w exeter-airport.co.uk
c 01392 367433

First Kernow
w firstgroup.com/cornwall
c 0345 602 0121

FlyBe
w flybe.com

Land's End Airport
w landsendairport.co.uk
c 01736 788771

Newquay Airport
w cornwallairportnewquay.com
c 01637 860600

Skybus
w islesofscilly-travel.co.uk/skybus

Stagecoach
w stagecoachbus.com

ARRIVING BY TRAIN

Great Western Railway
w gwr.com

ARRIVING BY ROAD

National Express
w nationalexpress.com

ARRIVING BY SEA

Brittany Ferries
w brittany-ferries.co.uk

Isles of Scilly Travel
w islesofscilly-travel.co.uk
c 01736 334220

Lundy Shore Office
w lundyisland.co.uk
c 01271 863636

GETTING AROUND BY BUS

Cornwall County Council
w cornwallpublictransport.info/bus_operators.asp
c 0300 1234 222

Devon County Council
w new.devon.gov.uk/travel/bus/bus-operators/
c 0345 155 1015

GETTING AROUND ON FOOT

South West Coast Path
w southwestcoastpath.org.uk

GETTING AROUND BY BIKE

National Cycle Network
w nationalcyclenetwork.org.uk

Sustrans
w sustrans.org.uk

GETTING AROUND BY RIVER FERRY

C Toms & Son
w ctomsandson.co.uk

King Harry
w falriver.co.uk

Kingswear Ferry
w dartmouthhigherferry.com

Mevagissey Ferries
w mevagissey-ferries.co.uk

Padstow Ferry
w padstow-harbour.co.uk

Practical Information

Passports and Visas

A valid passport or a national identity card issued by a European Economic Area (EEA) country or Switzerland is required to enter Britain. For stays shorter than 6 months, visitors from the US, Canada, New Zealand and Australia do not need visas to enter the country. EU citizens currently don't need visas and can stay as long as they like. Visitors from outside these zones should check with the British embassy in their home country or visit the **UK Government** website to find out more about their visa requirements or to apply for a visa. Most countries have consular representation in London, including the USA, Canada, New Zealand and Australia.

Customs Regulations and Immigration

Visitors from EU states can bring unlimited quantities of most goods into the UK for personal use without paying duty. Exceptions include illegal drugs, offensive weapons, endangered species and some types of food and plants. For more information about allowances from within and outside the EU, visit the UK Government website.

Travel Safety Advice

Visitors can get up-to-date travel safety information from the **UK Foreign and Commonwealth Office**, the **US Department of State** and the **Australian Department of Foreign Affairs and Trade**.

Travel Insurance

It is advisable to take out an insurance policy that covers theft, loss of baggage, cancellations and medical treatment. Some policies also cover injuries sustained in dangerous sports – check with your insurance company for details.

Health

No vaccinations are mandatory before visiting the UK. For police, fire or ambulance services call the **Emergency Number**; the operator will ask you which service you require. At the time of publication, free **National Health Service (NHS)** emergency treatment was available to visitors, but in the future patients may need to show ID before treatment. There are a number of hospitals in the region with 24-hour emergency services. **Plymouth Derriford Hospital**, Exeter's **Royal Devon & Exeter Hospital** and the **Royal Cornwall Hospital Trust** in Truro are the main hospitals.

If you need medical help but the situation is not an emergency, call the **NHS 111 Service**.

In all cases, specialist medical care, drugs and repatriation are costly. Keep all receipts for reimbursement from your insurance provider.

Pharmacies are open during business hours, some until late, and staff can give advice on minor ailments. **Boots** is a large national chain with a number of branches in towns throughout Cornwall and Devon.

Hotels can usually suggest local dentists, and many are listed in the Yellow Pages. You can also search for a nearby GP, dentist or pharmacy on the NHS website.

Personal Security

Theft and violent crime are rare in Cornwall and Devon. Take normal precautions about locking your car and not leaving bags unattended. Report any theft to the police immediately, as you will need a crime report number to make an insurance claim.

To avoid unwanted confrontation it's best to avoid the pubbing areas in Newquay, Torquay and Plymouth after dark at weekends. If you suffer any trouble or aggression, report it to the police.

Weather, Winds and Tides

The best times to visit Cornwall and Devon are in spring and autumn – weather in September and October is regularly better than it is in August. However, the weather, as throughout the UK, is unpredictable. The narrowness of the peninsula means that weather conditions here can change with alarming rapidity. Hikers especially can run into danger by being caught unawares. Make sure you check the weather forecast on TV and radio, in newspapers, at tourist offices or on the website of the **British Meteorological Office**.

The tide comes in very fast, and beach walkers have been cut off or drowned in the past – always check the tide tables before heading out. They are prominently displayed in coastal towns and villages, and can be checked online on the **BBC**, **Beach Guide** or **Windfinder** websites.

Travellers with Special Needs

Provision for visitors with special needs are steadily improving in Cornwall and Devon. Hotels, restaurants and museums with lifts and ramps for wheelchair access are becoming more common across the region, as are accessible buses.

Assistance is available for rail travellers – best arranged in advance – though some small stations are unstaffed. The **National Rail** website lists all train stations on the national network, with details of accessibility and whether assistance can be requested.

Banks, post offices, theatres, museums and many other public places provide aids for the visually- or hearing-impaired – although you may need to ask for hearing loops to be switched on.

The national charity Tourism for All has an excellent website called **Open Britain**, which has information on accommodation, attractions, shops, transport and places to eat. **Countryside Mobility South West** is a not-for-profit organization that rents mobility equipment – all-terrain trampers – at several sites. They also have wheelyboats for hire at several inland lakes.

Time Difference

The UK is on Greenwich Mean Time (GMT) from late October to late March. For the rest of the year it operates on British Summer Time (BST), which is one hour ahead of GMT. GMT is five hours ahead of US Eastern Standard Time and one hour behind Central European Time.

Electrical Appliances

Electricity in the UK is 230 volts 50 Hz. Plugs have three square pins; most overseas visitors will need a plug adaptor. North American visitors will need a converter too.

DIRECTORY

PASSPORTS & VISAS

UK Government
🆆 gov.uk

TRAVEL SAFETY ADVICE

Australian Department of Foreign Affairs and Trade
🆆 dfat.gov.au
🆆 smartraveller.gov.au

UK Foreign and Commonwealth Office
🆆 www.gov.uk/
foreign-travel-advice

US Department of State
🆒 travel.state.gov

HEALTH

Boots
🆆 boots.com

Emergency Number
🆒 999

National Health Service (NHS)
🆆 nhs.uk

NHS 111 Service
🆒 111

Plymouth Derriford Hospital
🆆 plymouthhospitals.
nhs.uk

Royal Cornwall Hospital Trust
🆆 royalcornwall.nhs.uk

Royal Devon & Exeter Hospital
🆆 rdehospital.nhs.uk

WEATHER, WINDS AND TIDES

BBC
🆆 bbc.co.uk/weather/
coast_and_sea/tide_
tables

Beach Guide
🆆 thebeachguide.co.uk

British Meteorological Office
🆆 metoffice.gov.uk/
public/weather/forecast

Windfinder
🆆 windfinder.com

TRAVELLERS WITH SPECIAL NEEDS

Countryside Mobility South West
🆆 countrysidemobility.
org

National Rail
🆆 nationalrail.co.uk/
stations_destinations

Open Britain
🆆 openbritain.net

Currency and Banking

The pound sterling is divided into 100 pence (p). Notes come in denominations of £5, £10, £20 and £50. Coins are 1p, 2p, 5p, 10p, 20p, 50p, £1 and £2. Virtually all banks have 24-hour external cash machines (ATMs).

Main branches of the **Post Office** change money for no commission and there are regulated bureaux de change.

Chip and Pin and contactless cards are generally accepted and most places take credit cards, most commonly **MasterCard** and **Visa**; **American Express** less so.

Opening Hours

Major supermarkets are generally open 8am–8pm. Other shops usually open between 9am and 10am and close at 5 or 5:30pm. On Sundays, all shops (except for small food shops) are restricted to opening for only six hours, generally 10am–4pm.

Banks usually open 9am or 9:30am to 3:30 or 4pm weekdays. Some branches also open on Saturday mornings. Museums usually open between 9am and 10am, closing between 4 and 6pm.

Telephone and Internet

Most hotels, B&Bs and restaurants provide free Wi-Fi. Mobile coverage is patchy, and public phones are rare. Visitors from abroad should check their provider's roaming rates; it can be cheaper to buy a SIM card in the UK. If you have Wi-Fi coverage, apps such as **Skype**, **Viber** and **WhatsApp** are useful for making calls.

Area codes are always dialled. When calling from abroad, first dial the international access code, then the area code, omitting the initial 0. To call abroad, dial 00 then the access code.

TV, Radio and Newspapers

Regional newspapers, such as the *Western Morning News*, the *Cornishman* and *West Briton*, publish detailed events listings and provide information on local closures, road-works, tide times and the weather. Magazines such as *Cornwall Life* and *Devon Life* are useful for cultural coverage.

Local TV and radio cover regional events, traffic and the weather. Tune in to **BBC Radio Devon** and **BBC Radio Cornwall** or commercial stations such as **Pirate FM** and **Radio Plymouth**.

Postal Services

Post offices are scattered throughout the region and you can buy stamps at many newsagents. Post offices and the **Royal Mail** website provide details on postal charges. For UK destinations, letters can be sent first class for next-day delivery or second-class for delivery within three working days.

Sources of Information

The official tourist board websites **Visit Devon** and **Visit Cornwall** are an excellent first stop for information, and they provide details of all the region's visitor centres.

The **Dartmoor National Park** and **Exmoor National Park** websites list details of their network of visitor centres, which have useful information and books and maps on the area.

Trips and Tours

Scores of national and local companies organize walking holidays in Devon and Cornwall, several focusing on the **South West Coast Path** *(see pp110–11)*. The tourist board and SWCP websites list operators. Other organized holiday options include cycling tours run by **Devon by Bike** or **Cornish Cycle Tours**. **Rick Stein** runs classic fish and seafood cooking courses, while the **Sharpham Trust** focuses on cooking and mindfulness, and **Manna from Devon** on cooking in a wood-fired oven. The **Newlyn Art School** and **Coombe Farm Studios** run art holidays, and bushcraft adventures for children and adults are organized by **Wildwise** and **Serious Outdoor Skills**.

Shopping

There are few shopping malls in Devon and a plethora of independent shops thrive among familiar chains, reflecting the distinct characters of the region, with beach and surf clothes, and scores of galleries and interiors shops inspired by the area. Watersports and sailing gear includes locally manufactured **Gul** wetsuits and snorkels and **Finisterre** clothing.

Devon has some excellent Farmers Markets, and delis throughout the region sell great local vegetables, meats and cheeses. Beers brewed locally are available, as is local gin from **Plymouth Gin**, vodka from **Aval Dor** and spiced rum from **Dead Man's Fingers**.

Dining

Places to eat range from nationally recognized Michelin-starred restaurants to local bakeries selling Cornish pasties, the emphasis always on local produce served in a relaxed, informal setting. Nearly all restaurants are family-friendly, if only at certain times of day.

Local lobster, crab, shellfish, oysters and wetfish dominate coastal menus, while rural Devon has grass-fed rare-breeds of meat. The most famous cheeses are Cornish Yarg and Davidstow Cheddar. Clotted cream features famously in the counties' rival cream teas, but also in local ice cream.

Tipping is expected only if service is not included.

Where to Stay

Devon and Cornwall have a vast range of accommodation to meet all needs, budgets and tastes. There are grand Victorian seaside hotels, hip country retreats, trendy B&Bs, camp sites and caravan sites. Self-catering options have been expanded by owner-led sites such as **Airbnb**. For the best rates, use broker sites such as **Booking.com**, **Kayak** and **Expedia**, and check the offers available on the hotel's own website.

DIRECTORY

CURRENCY AND BANKING

American Express
w americanexpress.com/uk

MasterCard
w mastercard.co.uk

Post Office
w postoffice.co.uk

Visa
w visa.co.uk

TELEPHONE AND INTERNET

Skype
w skype.com

Viber
w viber.com

WhatsApp
w whatsapp.com

TV, RADIO AND NEWSPAPERS

BBC Radio Cornwall
w bbc.co.uk/radiocornwall

BBC Radio Devon
w bbc.co.uk/radiodevon

Cornishman
w cornwalllive.com

Cornwall Life
w cornwalllife.co.uk

Devon Life
w devonlife.co.uk

Pirate FM
w piratefm.co.uk

Radio Plymouth
w radioplymouth.com

West Briton
w cornwalllive.com

Western Morning News
w devonlive.com

POSTAL SERVICES

Royal Mail
w royalmail.com

SOURCES OF INFORMATION

Dartmoor National Park
w dartmoor-npa.gov.uk

Exmoor National Park
w exmoor-nationalpark.gov.uk

Visit Cornwall
w visitcornwall.com

Visit Devon
w visitdevon.co.uk

TRIPS AND TOURS

Coombe Farm Studios
w coombefarmstudios.com

Cornish Cycle Tours
w cornishcycletours.co.uk

Devon by Bike
w devonbybike.co.uk

Manna from Devon
w mannafromdevon

Newlyn Art School
w newlynartschool.co.uk

Rick Stein
w rickstein.com

Serious Outdoor Skills
w seriousoutdoorskills.co.uk

Sharpham Trust
w sharphamtrust.org

South West Coast Path
w southwestcoastpath.org.uk

Wildwise
w wildwise.co.uk

SHOPPING

Aval Dor
w aval-dor.co.uk

Dead Man's Fingers
w cornishron.com

Finisterre
w finisterre.com

Gul
w gul.com

Plymouth Gin
w plymouthgin.com

WHERE TO STAY

Airbnb
w airbnb.co.uk

Booking.com
w booking.com

Expedia
w expedia.co.uk

Kayak
w kayak.co.uk

Places to Stay

PRICE CATEGORIES
For a standard, double room per night (with breakfast if included), taxes and extra charges.

£ under £100 ££ £100–£200 £££ over £200

COASTAL

Boscastle YHA
MAP D2 ■ Palace Stables, Boscastle ■ 0845 3719006 ■ www.yha.org.uk ■ £
Set right on Boscastle's quayside, this hostel has dorms, private rooms with en suite facilities and a four-bed room with its own bathroom and kitchen. Perfect for walks on the South West Coast Path.

Lizard YHA
MAP C6 ■ Lizard Point ■ 0845 371 9550 ■ www.yha.org.uk ■ £
Located on Britain's most southerly point, this hostel occupies a former four-star Victorian hotel. Choose between dorm rooms or bigger family rooms, many with sea views. There's a kitchen, sitting room and garden.

Lundy House Hotel
MAP H1 ■ Chapel Hill, Mortehoe ■ 01271 870372 ■ www.lundyhousehotel. webvilla.net ■ £
Each one of the eight rooms is different at this B&B overlooking Woolacombe Bay. Great sea views accompany the hearty breakfasts. There is a family room and a self-catering apartment.

Norbury House
MAP H1 ■ Torrs Park, Ilfracombe ■ 01271 863888 ■ www.norbury house.co.uk ■ £
Contemporary rooms in a stylish Victorian B&B overlooking the sea. Visitors can help themselves to drinks in the cocktail bar, or tea and biscuits in the lounge.

The Beach
MAP E2 ■ Summerleaze Crescent, Bude ■ 01288 389800 ■ www.thebeach atbude.co.uk ■ ££
This lively seaside hotel, features a very cool bar with a decked terrace overlooking the beach, and rooms with limed oak furniture and king-size beds. Popular with surfers.

Hell Bay
MAP A4 ■ Bryher, Isles of Scilly ■ 01720 422947 ■ www.hellbay.co.uk ■ ££-£££
This chic, contemporary hotel is set above a rugged bay on tiny, remote Bryher island. There's an outdoor heated swimming pool, some fabulous art and locally sourced food in the informal restaurant. It's excellent for families: a games room has table football, a pool table, a TV and video games, including an outdoor play area.

The Old Quay House
MAP E4 ■ Fore St, Fowey ■ 01726 833302 ■ theold quayhouse.com ■ ££
This elegant hotel is set in a whitewashed Victorian building on the banks of the River Fowey. Some of its bedrooms have balconies that overlook the estuary. No children under 12.

Old Success Inn
MAP A5 ■ Cove Hill, Sennen Cove ■ 01736 871232 ■ www.old success.co.uk ■ ££
An unpretentious seaside pub right on Sennen Cove, with rooms decorated in Cornish coastal style. Rooms feature plantation shutters and furnishings in calming shades of sand, pebble and blue. This cosy pub also has a great terrace.

Pedn Olva
MAP B5 ■ West Porthminster Beach, St Ives ■ 01736 796222 ■ www.pednolva.co.uk ■ ££
Set on the cliffs between the beaches at St Ives, Pedn Olva has a chic boutique feel. Many rooms have balconies, and there are terraces for alfresco drinking, or for wallowing in the plunge pool. An informal restaurant serves Modern British food.

Red Lion
MAP G2 ■ The Quay, Clovelly ■ 01237 431237 ■ www.stayatclovelly. co.uk/red-lion ■ ££
A welcoming inn with cosy rooms and lovely views of Clovelly's picturesque harbour, plus superior renditions of traditional pub grub. The Sail Loft annexe has larger bedrooms with sea views that cost only a fraction more.

Rosevine
MAP C5 ■ Rosevine, Nr Portscatho ■ 01872 580206 ■ www.rosevine.co.uk ■ ££
A country house by the sea that combines both the comforts of a luxury

hotel with the independence of self-catering. Set in luxuriant gardens above a sheltered sandy cove, it has a playroom, an indoor heated pool, an adults-only lounge and a restaurant. The studios, apartments and suites all have a kitchen and dining area.

St Petroc's
MAP D3 ▪ New St, Padstow ▪ 01841 532700 ▪ www.rickstein.com ▪ ££
A sociable little town house hotel above a buzzy Rick Stein bistro and bar, with a labyrinth of stylish sitting and reading rooms. The ten bedrooms are not huge, but are very comfortable, and have a nautical New England style.

Soar Mill Cove
MAP J6 ▪ Soar Mill Cove, Salcombe ▪ 01548 561566 ▪ www.soarmillcove.co.uk ▪ ££
Set in its very own cove, a short drive from Salcombe, this friendly hotel has been in the same family for three generations. There's plenty to entertain adults and kids, with an indoor saltwater pool, tennis court, games room, great food and a champagne bar. The beach and rock pools are on the doorstep.

Victoria House
MAP H1 ▪ Chapel Hill, Mortehoe ▪ 01271 871302 ▪ www.victoriahousebandb.co.uk ▪ ££
An elegant Edwardian B&B with sea views from every room. The beach house has its own private deck. This is a tranquil place aimed at adults (no toddlers),

with the beach right on the doorstep.

Watergate Bay Hotel
MAP C4 ▪ Watergate Bay ▪ 01637 860543 ▪ www.watergatebay.co.uk ▪ ££-£££
Watergate Bay is a prime surfing location and this contemporary hotel has a very relaxed beachside vibe. Extreme Academy here is one of the best watersports schools in the country. Self-catering is available.

Burgh Island Hotel
MAP J6 ▪ Burgh Island, Bigbury-on-Sea ▪ 01548 810514 ▪ www.burghisland.com ▪ £££
Art Deco elegance on an island reached by a tidal causeway. Former guests include Winston Churchill, Noël Coward and Agatha Christie. There's a 1930s billiards room, cocktail bar and swimming lagoon. Murder mystery parties are regularly hosted.

Idle Rocks
MAP C5 ▪ Harbourside, St Mawes ▪ 01326 270270 ▪ www.idlerocks.com ▪ £££
A lovely conversion of an Edwardian waterfront inn, in chic St Mawes. The interior here is fabulous, adorned with driftwood sculptures, collections of vintage bathing suits and the like. The hotel restaurant uses the freshest local ingredients and the south facing terrace is perfect for admiring the view.

The Nare
MAP C5 ▪ Veryan-in-Roseland ▪ 01872 501111 ▪ www.narehotel.co.uk ▪ £££
A family-run country house on the Roseland

Peninsula, with warm, traditional styling – plenty of antiques and heirlooms. Spectacular views can be had from the relaxed Quarterdeck and the more formal dining room. There's also an outdoor swimming pool and a private launch. It's ideal for families with children, particularly as it has direct beach access.

St Edmunds
MAP D3 ▪ St Edmunds Ln, Padstow ▪ 01841 532700 ▪ www.rickstein.com ▪ £££
A refined Padstow retreat in an elegant town house with a garden and views over the estuary – just a couple of minutes' walk from all the Rick Stein restaurants. Designed by Jill Stein, these are the most luxurious of the Stein rooms, with oak floors, French windows, plantation shutters and bespoke oak furniture.

St Enodoc
MAP D3 ▪ Rock ▪ 01208 863394 ▪ www.enodoc-hotel.co.uk ▪ £££
One of Cornwall's pioneering seaside chic hotels, set in spacious grounds right next to a golf course, across the river from Padstow (and reached by passenger ferry). Rooms are modern with a cosy Scandinavian theme, and many have extensive estuary views. There's a spa, a beach on the doorstep, and the hotel is very family-friendly. Chef Nathan Outlaw cooked here until recently – the kitchen has now been taken over by Masterchef winner James Nathan.

The Scarlet

MAP C4 ▪ Tredragon Rd, Mawgan Porth ▪ 01637 861800 ▪ www.scarlet hotel.co.uk ▪ £££

This super-indulgent, super-chic, eco hotel is embedded in the cliffs above Mawgan Porth beach. There are log-fired hot tubs, an Ayurvedic spa, a natural swimming pool, and a restaurant serving Modern European food using local produce. It's strictly for grown-ups only, and is the ultimate romantic retreat.

South Sands Hotel

MAP J6 ▪ Bolt Head, Salcombe ▪ 01548 845 900 ▪ www.southsands. com ▪ £££

Waves practically lap right up to this New England-style contemporary hotel. It has a grand spiral staircase and an excellent restaurant. The blue and white theme with nautical touches runs throughout the 22 bedrooms.

Tresanton

MAP C5 ▪ 27 Lower Castle Rd, St Mawes ▪ 01326 270055 ▪ www.tresanton. com ▪ £££

Created by Olga Polizzi within the buildings of a 1940s yacht club, this hotel has sweeping views across the bay to St Anthony's lighthouse. The hotel's wooden yacht, *Pinuccia*, is available for skippered sails around the sheltered waters of the Fal Estuary and Helford River.

COUNTRY

Broomhill Art Hotel

MAP H2 ▪ Muddiford, Barnstaple ▪ 01271 850262 ▪ www.broomhill art.co.uk ▪ £

A unique hotel – its eight individually styled rooms are set in a Victorian house surrounded by a contemporary sculpture garden. The Terra Madre restaurant serves Mediterranean food.

East Dyke Farmhouse

MAP G2 ▪ Higher Clovelly ▪ 01237 431216 ▪ £

A 15-minute walk above the honeypot of Clovelly, this 200-year-old farmhouse offers three spacious bedrooms of which two have splendid sea-views. Breakfast is served in the lovely flagstoned dining room.

Keynedon Mill

MAP J6 ▪ Sherford, Kingsbridge ▪ 01548 531485 ▪ www.keynedon mill.co.uk ▪ £

A stylish B&B occupying an ancient stone mill, furnished with French rustic antiques, vintage finds and comfy modern furniture. Children under 12 are not allowed to stay.

Okehampton YHA

MAP H3 ▪ Klondyke Rd, Okehampton ▪ 01837 53916 ▪ www.yha.org.uk ▪ £

Set in a converted railway goods shed on the northern edge of Dartmoor, this hostel caters to various pursuits, including rock climbing, abseiling, gorge scrambling, geocaching and pony trekking.

Zennor Chapel

MAP A5 ▪ Zennor, St Ives ▪ 01736 798307 ▪ www. zennorchapel guesthouse.com ▪ £

This old Methodist chapel, located in the village where D H Lawrence once lived, has five comfortable rooms and is close to the South West Coast Path. There is a café attached serving home-made food, plus a gift shop. There's also a regular bus service to the town of St Ives.

Cider House

MAP H5 ▪ Buckland Abbey, Yelverton ▪ 01822 259062 ▪ www.cider-house.co.uk ▪ ££

This boutique B&B is located on the 700-acre estate of Buckland Abbey, occupying the building where the monks used to make cider. Guests have access to the estate and abbey with waymarked trails, and to the kitchen gardens, hens and beehives. There is also glamping in two super-stylish shepherds' huts.

Coombeshead Farm

MAP E3 ▪ Lewannick ▪ 01566 782009 ▪ www. coombesheadfarm.co.uk ▪ ££

The perfect farmstay for sociable foodies, run by two chefs in a Georgian farmhouse surrounded by 66 acres of woodland and meadows, with kitchen gardens, hens, beehives, a wood oven, firepit and more. Rooms are simple and comfy, and every evening a communal three-course dinner is served using the farm's own livestock, vegetables and foraged foods. No under-12s.

Hotel Endsleigh

MAP H4 ▪ Milton Abbot, Tavistock ▪ 01822 870000 ▪ www.hotelendsleigh. com ▪ ££

A stylish country house hotel created by Olga

Polizzi in a 19th-century hunting lodge in the glorious Tamar Valley. The grounds were landscaped by Sir Humphry Repton and cover 100 acres of formal gardens, streams, woodlands, follies and grottoes. The house retains many original features and is decorated with a seamless fusion of old and new, including walk-in showers and large, comfortable beds.

The Old Rectory
MAP D2 ▪ St Juliot, Boscastle ▪ 01840 250225 ▪ Closed Dec–mid-Feb ▪ www.stjuliot.com ▪ ££
The writer Thomas Hardy once stayed in this rural guesthouse located on Boscastle's outskirts. All rooms are preserved in their Victorian splendour and there are some lovely wooded gardens. Children under 12 are not allowed.

Gidleigh Park
MAP J4 ▪ Chagford ▪ 01647 432367 ▪ www.gidleigh.co.uk ▪ £££
A romantic haven in a striking half-timbered Tudor-style house set amid 107 acres of private woodland in Dartmoor National Park. The style is traditional, with plenty of antiques, while the restaurant here is one of the region's most exceptional (see p60).

TOWN

Falmouth Lodge Backpackers
MAP C5 ▪ Gyllyngvase Terrace, Falmouth ▪ 01326 319996 ▪ www.falmouthbackpackers.co.uk ▪ £
This homely hostel, in an Edwardian half-timbered

semi-detached house, is just a street away from Gyllyngvase beach, with a comfy living room, a conservatory, kitchen, and outdoor spaces. There are six rooms, three of which can be rented as dorms or family rooms, two doubles or twins, and an en suite attic room. Bookings by phone only.

Highcliffe
MAP C5 ▪ 22 Melvill Rd, Falmouth ▪ 01326 314466 ▪ www.highcliffefalmouth.com ▪ £
Engaging owners and fantastic breakfasts feature at this boutique B&B on a quiet residential road between the estuary and the sea. Beaches and the town are within easy walking distance, and there are views from the rooms at the back, over the roofscape of Victorian Falmouth to the estuary.

Penzance YHA
MAP B5 ▪ Castle Horneck, Penzance ▪ 08453 719653 ▪ www.yha.org.uk/hostel/penzance ▪ £
A well-equipped hostel occupying a Georgian mansion just 15 minutes' walk from the centre of Penzance. Within its beautiful grounds are a barbecue area and a camp site. Open all year, it has a self-catering kitchen and dining room, plus bunks, double and family rooms.

Chapel House PZ
MAP B5 ▪ Chapel St, Penzance ▪ 01736 362024 ▪ www.chapelhousepz.co.uk ▪ ££
This Georgian town house with views across the bay to St Michael's Mount is furnished with a mix of

antiques and iconic 20th-century designer pieces, set off by subtle grey floorboards and antique kilim rugs.

The Greenbank
MAP C5 ▪ Harbourside, Falmouth ▪ 01326 312440 ▪ www.greenbank-hotel.co.uk ▪ ££
Set on the banks of the Fal, this hotel has evolved over 400 years, with its 50 rooms across four interlinked buildings. The lounge-bar is the perfect place to sit, and there are two outdoor terraces, as well as the popular Working Boat pub.

Southernhay House
MAP K3 ▪ 36 Southernhay East, Exeter ▪ 01392 439000 ▪ www.southernhayhouse.com ▪ ££
This luxurious town house hotel in the city's Georgian quarter features monsoon showers and mid-room rolltop baths, giving the rooms a boudoir feel. There's also a cocktail bar and a restaurant.

Star Castle
MAP B4 ▪ St Mary's, Isles of Scilly ▪ 01720 422317 ▪ www.star-castle.co.uk ▪ ££–£££
This star-shaped fortress, built at the order of Elizabeth I, has fantastic views from its turrets and ramparts. Inside, it's all wood-beamed ceilings, creaky staircases, and crooked rooms furnished with a miscellany of Persian rugs, Jacobean-style furniture, and comfy old sofas. There are more conventional, spacious rooms in the castle garden, along with a lovely indoor pool.

For a key to hotel price categories see p116

Index

Acknowledgments

Author

Robert Andrews has been travelling and writing travel guidebooks for 20 years. His main areas of interest are the West Country in England and southern Italy. Based in Bristol, he also writes articles, compiles anthologies and takes photographs.

Additional contributor
Ros Belford

Publishing Director Georgina Dee

Publisher Vivien Antwi

Design Director Phil Ormerod

Editorial Sophie Adam, Ankita Awasthi Tröger, Kate Berens, Rachel Fox, Lucy Richards, Sally Schafer, Anuroop Sanwalia

Cover Design Richard Czapnik

Design Tessa Bindloss, Bharti Karakoti

Commissioned Photography Tim Draper, John Harrison, Nigel Hicks

Picture Research Subhadeep Biswas, Taiyaba Khatoon, Ellen Root, Rituraj Singh

Cartography Ashutosh Bharti, Suresh Kumar, James Macdonald, Casper Morris, John Plumer

Mapping based on data from the People's Map

DTP Jason Little

Production Igrain Roberts

Factchecker Kate Hughes

Proofreader Laura Walker

Indexer Hilary Bird

Picture Credits

The publisher would like to thank the following for their kind permission to reproduce their photographs:
Key: a-above; b-below/bottom; c-centre; f-far; l-left; r-right; t-top

123RF.com: Radomír Režný 63br.

4Corners: Pietro Canali 20–1, 52b, 53br, 62b, 102–3; Arcangelo Piai 79br; Dave Porter 82tl; Maurizio Rellini 24tr, 94cla, 96b.

Alamy Stock Photo: Herb Bendicks 73tr; Kevin Britland 4cla, 18–9, 34cla, 58tl, 64bl, 68bc, 107cra; Adam Burton 4crb; David Chapman 92c; E.J.Westmacott 35tc; Economic Images 58b; Greg Balfour Evans 32cl; Guy Edwardes Photography 81tl; Nick Hanna 3tr, 108–9; David Hastilow 34bl; Holmes Garden Photos 25tr; i on the world 28cb; Ian Dagnall Commercial Collection 93cr; incamerastock 29tl, 76b, 83bl; Interfoto/ Houses in St Ives (c.1940) by Alfred Wallis 49br; International Photobank 68tr; Christopher Jones 44t; Ian Kingsnorth 31crb; LatitudeStock 57cl; Geraint Lewis / Seed (2003–7) by Peter Randall-Page 14cb, Mary Evans Picture Library/ D H Lawrence by Jeffrey Morgan 48tl; Paul Melling 30bl; MSP Travel Images 61tr; The National Trust Photolibrary National Trust Images 96tl; Christopher Nicholson 59crb; David Pearson 4clb; Lee Pengelly 23cr; Will Perrett 26–7; Ben Ramos 100tl; Matthias Riedinger 106b; Robertharding 2tr, 36–7; Steve Taylor ARPS 11cra, 54tl, 62tl; Anna Stevenson 56br; Derek Stone 3tl, 66b, 70–1; Peter Titmuss 42b; VIEW Pictures Ltd 15tl; Paul Washer 4cl; Washington Imaging 75bl; Westmacott 40b; Jim Wileman 78tl.

AWL Images: Robert Birkby 73br, 101tr; Adam Burton 16–7, 29crb, 76cla; Danita Delimont Stock 103cl; Travel Pix Collection 11clb.

Depositphotos Inc: brians101 4cr; linfernum 12cl.

Dreamstime.com: Acceleratorhams 11crb, 55tr; Adeliepenguin 11cr; Alexirina27000 11b; Steve Allen 53cl; Gordon Bell 52tl; Dan Breckwoldt 4b; Clive Chilvers 69cl; Colinboylett 97cl; Darrensharvey 12–3; Davidmartyn 89tr; Deborahhelen 15cla; Dreambigphotos 65tr; Hannah6d 7br; Helen Hotson 10bl, 17tl, 38t, 46–7, 57tr, 66cla, 89bl; Darren Howe 74–5; Clare Jackson 104cl; Anthony Jacobs 58c; Valerijs Jegorovs 47cr; Johnhill118 102tr; Aagje De Jong 10cl, 14–5, 39tr, 67br; Keatsy3 56t; Denis Kelly 67tl; Shahid Khan 10crb; Lymey 33clb; Daniel Marsh 90c; Sue Martin 24bl; Chris Moncrieff 10tr, 13tl; Colin & Oksana Phillipson 51c, 90–1; Andrew Roland 26br; Sharpshot 6cla; Kiril Stanchev 98t; Stevieuk 13crb; Petr Švec 19crb; Jennifer Thompson 83cr; Vaclav Volrab 28cla; Ian Woolcock 11tl, 30–1, 33tl, 43crb, 86–7, 92b, 105b; Pavla Zakova 80–1.

Driftwood: 61clb.

English Heritage: Dorling Kindersley /Nigel Hicks 46tl.

Getty Images: AFP 49tl; Dave Porter Peterborough Uk 16bl; Andreas von Einsiedel 91bl; Fox Photos 48br; Franz-Marc Frei 27cra; Hulton Deutsch 39clb; Loop Images 84cla, / Sebastian Wasek 4t; James Osmond 54–5; Print Collector 38br; Olaf Protze 2tl, 8–9, 22br, 24c, 25bl, 32–3, 101br; Robertharding / Peter Barritt 27tl; Andy Sheppard 69br; Paul Thompson 14cla, 30crb; Peter Unger 88ca; Sebastian Wasek 17bc.

Gidleigh Park, Andrew Brownsword Hotels: 60t.

©HeliganGardensLtd: 50t.

iStockphoto.com: George Clerk 64tr; csfotoimages 74cl; RolfSt 1, 95t; George Standen 34–5.

Masons Arms: 60bl.

National Maritime Museum Cornwall: 19tl.

National Trust Images: Lynda Aiano 40ca, 44cb; Andrew Butler 50clb; Andreas von Einsiedel 12br; Angelo Hornak 45tr; John Millar 51tr.

Paignton Zoo Environmental Park: Ray Wiltshire 82c.

PENGUIN and the Penguin logo are trademarks of Penguin Books Ltd: *Lorna Doone* by R. D. Blackmore 48c.

Penlee House: 41tr.

Rex Shutterstock: Bill Bradshaw 80cl.

Robert Harding Picture Library: Ashley Cooper 28bl, 72cla; J. Kruse 79tr.

Rockfish: 85clb.

The Royal Cornwall Museum: 95br.

The St Mawes Hotel: David Griffen Photography 99clb.

SuperStock: age fotostock /Craig Joiner 16cl, /Olaf Protze 22cla, /Sebastian Wasek 35crb.

Trebah: David Chapman 18bl.

Cover

Front and spine: **4Corners:** Pietro Canali.

Back: **Dreamstime.com:** Fisfra

Pull Out Map Cover

4Corners: Pietro Canali.

All other images © Dorling Kindersley
For further information see:
www.dkimages.com

Printed and bound in China

First published in Great Britain in 2009
by Dorling Kindersley Limited
80 Strand, London WC2R 0RL

Copyright 2009, 2018 © Dorling
Kindersley Limited

A Penguin Random House Company

18 19 20 21 10 9 8 7 6 5 4 3 2 1

Reprinted with revisions 2011, 2013, 2015, 2018

A CIP catalogue record is available from the British Library.

ISBN 978 0 2413 0672 7

As a guide to abbreviations in visitor information blocks: **Adm** = *admission charge;* **DA** = *disabled access;* **D** = *dinner;* **L** = *lunch.*

Selected Town Index